## Also by Harriet and Shirley

***Glimpses of God: a winter devotional for women***

***Prayer Warrior Confessions***

***Glimpses of Prayer, a devotional***

***Glimpses of the Savior, a devotional***

### By Harriet

***Prayer, It's Not About You***

### By Shirley

***Study Guide on Prayer***

# Glimpses of God

## a summer devotional for women

Shirley Crowder
Harriet E. Michael

Shirley Crowder
1 Thess 2:8

*Glimpses of God: a summer devotional for women*

Chapter illustrations by Kristin Michael.
ISBN: 978-1-951602-04-8



Published by:

E Entrusted Books, an imprint of Write Integrity Press
PO Box 702852; Dallas, TX 75370
www.WriteIntegrity.com

Published in the United States of America

# Dedication

We dedicate this devotional to
our Christ-following Dads:
the Rev. Ray Crowder
whose love for God, his family,
and others all over the world,
combined with his passion to help others know how to
live out the Scripture,
was a model to Shirley and her siblings,
and countless people of all ages,
of how to love others and teach them God's truth,
and
Dr. Keith Edwards
who, like Luke, could be called
"the beloved Physician."
He was loved by so many whom he cared for and
healed. Harriet and her siblings thought
he was the smartest man on earth.
Among his many achievements
was teaching his children to love Jesus.

*And these words that I command you today*
*shall be on your heart.*
*You shall teach them diligently to your children,*
*and shall talk of them when you sit in your house,*
*and when you walk by the way, and when you lie down,*
*and when you rise.*
Deuteronomy 6:6-7

# Table of Contents

# Introduction

Creator God made the world in which we live. He placed the moon and stars in the sky, the rivers and ocean on the earth. He also created seasons throughout the year. Each season is defined by specific features and attributes that are common, although the degree varies depending on where a person lives. In winter, we think of cold weather; in spring, blooming flowers; in summer, warm weather; and in the fall, beautifully colored leaves.

As Christ-followers, we also experience spiritual seasons. These seasons do not come in order like seasons in nature, which come regularly without fail. Each spiritual season we experience is defined by certain features, too. In spiritual winter, we think of the coldness of our relationship with God; in spring, new growth; in summer, warmth and heat; in fall, shedding the old and preparing for difficult days ahead.

In the same way that nature's seasons serve a

purpose on earth, so do the seasons in our spiritual lives. God provides, cares for, and sustains the earth, and in His faithfulness, He does the same for us. Our responsibility is to be obedient to God's commands in the Bible and to cling to the truth that God is in control.

This devotional is focused on summer—both calendar and spiritual. Our spiritual summer is a time of growth, hard work, and relaxation as we nurture and care for the new things that were planted in our spiritual spring and allow them to ripen or mature.

We pray that as you read and meditate upon the Bible passages and truths in each devotional that you will catch glimpses of God in and through everything around you. How has He provided for you? How is He protecting you? How is He teaching you?

Chapter 1

# A Call to Remember

## Day 1: Memorial Day Thoughts

by Harriet
Read Romans 13:1-7

*Give to everyone what you owe them:*
*if you owe taxes, pay taxes;*
*if revenue, then revenue; if respect, then respect;*
*if honor, then honor.*
Romans 13:7 (NIV)

Memorial Day is usually the kick-off for summer. We get a day off from work or school, swimming pools open in most places, and we enjoy the sunshine and warming temperatures. We celebrate with picnics or burgers grilled in our backyards. But what are we celebrating? To many of us who have never lost a friend or family member in the armed forces, we tend to fall into the idea that we are celebrating the start of summer. Nothing could be further from the truth.

Memorial Day is a call to remember. In particular, it's a call to remember those who gave their lives fighting for or defending our country.

Originally known as Decoration Day, Memorial Day began in the years following the Civil War as a time to decorate the graves of soldiers lost in that war. The Civil War claimed more lives than any other conflict in American history. It ended in 1865, and by the late 1860s Americans in various places began holding springtime tributes to the fallen soldiers—their brothers, sons, fathers—whom they loved very much and had lost in the war. These tributes included decorating the gravesites with spring flowers as well as poems and other small ceremonies to remember the fallen.

Though this practice started spontaneously in various places, Waterloo, New York, is considered the birthplace of Memorial Day because it began this celebration, which it called Decoration Day, on May 5, 1866, as a community-wide event with businesses closing so that the people could use the day to decorate the graves with flags and flowers. It became an official national holiday in 1971 with the last Monday in May named as the time to observe this new official holiday which was now called Memorial Day.

The Bible instructs us to remember things many times. Most often it tells us to remember God and to recall how He has worked in our lives and the blessings He has given to us, as well as who He is, His attributes, character traits, power, and ability to help us and to deliver us from our adversity. But, the Bible also speaks of remembering people. Two of my favorite verses that speak to this are Ephesians 1:16 (NIV) where it says, "I have not stopped giving thanks for you, remembering you in my prayers," and Philippians 1:3 (NIV), "I thank God every time I remember you."

My challenge to you today is to spend some time remembering. Be especially mindful of the brave men and women who fought to preserve our freedom. Those of us who live in the United States are blessed indeed. May we never take our freedoms for granted.

Let's also remember the men and women who went before us in faith touching our lives and those of others for the gospel of Jesus Christ. That is a battlefield, too, with a very real enemy. Many have sacrificed much for the cause of Christ; may we never forget that either.

**Prayer:** Heavenly Father, on this holiday weekend, as we enjoy the warm sunshine, the promise of summer days to come, fellowship with our family and friends, good food, and fun times, bring to our memories those who have sacrificed that we may enjoy such things. In Jesus' name, amen.

**Thought for the Day:** Our freedom cost others much; some even their lives. Likewise, though salvation is free to us, it cost Jesus everything.

## Day 2: Noble Sacrifice

by Shirley
Read John 15:12-17

*Greater love has no one than this,*
*that someone lay down his life for his friends.*
John 15:13

This time of year we see many pictures of all the gravestones at Arlington National Cemetery, each one with an American flag in front of it. This cemetery is the burial place for hundreds of thousands of service members who were in active duty, veterans, and some of their families. The Tomb of the Unknown Soldier is a monument to the US Armed Forces members whose remains have never been identified.

As Americans, we pause for a moment when we think of or view these hallowed grounds of burial. There is a tug on our heartstrings that reminds us of the thousands of men and women who have fought in all of the US wars. Hopefully, there is also a recognition of the sacred trust their sacrifice gave us.

What is that sacred trust? Our freedoms. Sadly, we often take these freedoms—purchased by the blood of those who died that we might live in freedom—for granted. Their noble sacrifice and heroism stand in stark contrast to the "look out for me" attitude that seems to permeate our current culture.

Because so many died for America and our freedoms, we must each dedicate ourselves to live for America—to make her a stronger nation of freedom—so that they would not have died in vain.

While the sacrifices of our service men and women were great as they fought in many battles, God's Son died on a cross, winning the battle against the evil one. Although His death may have seemed like defeat, through His death, burial, and resurrection, He paid the penalty for our sin and took upon Himself the punishment we deserve. Through the shed blood of Jesus Christ, the greatest sacrifice ever, our freedom from sin and eternal salvation was bought. The victory cry of His battle was, "It is finished" (John 19:30). This meant Jesus had completed all that His Father had given Him to do—and had reconciled sinful man to Himself.

As we remember the sacrifice of the service men and women, we must continue to work together as a nation united to protect our freedoms so that generations to come can enjoy the same freedoms.

As we remember the sacrifice of Jesus, we must strive to live our lives in obedience to His commands and for His glory. That can only happen when we come to a saving knowledge of Him through the regeneration of our hearts. That transforms us so that we can be ambassadors for Him by sharing the gospel with all those whom we come in contact. Real, lasting peace and freedom can only come through a relationship with Jesus.

**Prayer:** Heavenly Father, thank You for the freedoms Americans enjoy because of the sacrifice of the many service men and women who fought. Thank You for the sacrifice of Jesus on the cross that bought our freedom from sin. Help us to know You better so that we will be better equipped to serve You as we share Your sacrificial love to all those whom You bring across our paths. In Jesus' name, amen.

**Thought for the Day:** As you go through the day, give thanks to the Lord for the freedom Christ's sacrifice secured for you and for the freedoms you enjoy as an American.

## Day 3: In Flanders Fields

by Harriet
Read 1 Thessalonians 4:13-18

*Precious in the sight of the Lord*
*is the death of his saints.*
Psalm 116:15

"In Flanders Fields the poppies blow
Between the crosses, row on row,
That mark our place, and in the sky,
The larks still bravely singing fly,
Scarce heard amid the guns below."

Have you ever lost a loved one? This poem, familiar to most of us, was written by a Canadian physician, Lieutenant-Colonel John McCrae, on May 3, 1915, after he had presided over the funeral of friend and fellow soldier Lieutenant Alexis Helmer, who died in battle. The poignant second verse goes like this:

> "We are the dead; short days ago
> We lived, felt dawn, saw sunset glow,
> Loved and were loved, and now we lie
> In Flanders Fields."

One of my sons lost his best friend when he was only sixteen. Zack, the friend, had not quite turned sixteen yet when he crossed a busy road on his way to a Mexican restaurant from an indoor soccer club where he had just played, and was struck by a car and killed instantly. Like John McCrae, my son, too, recorded his thoughts. However, my son wrote a paragraph instead of a poem and his tribute did not become famous, though it was included on a tribute page in his high school yearbook. Here are my son's words:

> The best way I can describe my relationship with Zack would be to say he was my shadow. Not that I was some big influence, or that he followed me everywhere. But that no matter what happened, I would be able to look behind me and see him, smiling back at

> me. He would be so close to me when I'd fallen, that I could look him in the eye as he told me to get up, and he would be beside me as I was running, yelling, "I betcha I'm faster." And the same goes from me to him. That's how it was . . . and that's how it is. I can say the feeling of having him gone is as if my shadow disappeared. I can't explain what it feels like to have a part of me I never thought I'd lose become something I will never see again. So now, as I look back and no longer see my shadow, my friend, my brother, I can only imagine what is to come as I stare down the setting sun. But with every sunrise comes a new shadow. Unable to replace the first, but able to make the sun bearable again.

My son's message offers some hope at the end—a hope of getting past his grief, a hope of new friends to come, and a hope of seeing his friend Zack again. My son had these hopes because he knew his friend, like him, was a believer.

Paul, in 1 Corinthians 15:55, poses the question, "O death, where is your victory? O death, where is your sting?" It answers this question in the next few verses when it says in 56-57, "The sting of death is sin, and the power of sin is the law. But thanks be to God, who gives us victory through our Lord Jesus Christ."

Through Christ we have victory over sin, over the law, and over death itself.

**Prayer:** Almighty God, You have overcome sin and death. Thank You that through You we are granted everlasting life and because of that, we will not remain separated forever from other believers that we have loved and lost. In Jesus' name, amen.

**Thought for the Day:** This life is not all there is. We look forward to our eternal life, even as we remember those who have gone on before us.

## Day 4: Remember the Past for the Present and Future

by Shirley
Read 1 Corinthians 11:23-28

*For as often as you eat this bread and drink this cup, you proclaim the Lord's death until he comes.*
1 Corinthians 11:26

As a nation, we celebrate and remember those who fought for and helped keep the freedoms we enjoy today. Memorial Day is a time to pause as we remember, with thankfulness, those who gave their lives to secure and maintain our freedoms. We also remember the ideal on which our nation was founded and has stood through the years—liberty.

Together we have dealt with attacks and challenges, both foreign and domestic. Our deep love for America and all she stands for emboldens us to stand together, despite our differences, in the same way those whom we remember on Memorial Day stood firm in their resolve to defend our nation and her ideals.

One of the many Memorial Day traditions I love is how the flag of the United States is rapidly raised to full-staff and then somberly lowered to half-staff until noon in remembrance and honor of those who gave their lives in service to our nation. After noon, and for the balance of the day, the flag is raised to full-staff as a sign of our present determination to continue standing firm as we persist in defending our nation and her ideals.

While remembering the past, we look to the future and the continuation of our nation that allows her people to live in freedom. Ideally, all Americans would live together in freedom. That is the goal for which we strive as we fight against those who would destroy our freedom.

President Andrew Jackson, in his farewell address to the nation on March 4, 1837, said,

> Providence has showered on this favored land blessings without number, and has chosen you, as the guardians of freedom, to preserve it for the benefit of the human race. May He who holds in His hands the destinies of nations make

> you worthy of the favors He has bestowed, and enable you, with pure hearts, and pure hands, and sleepless vigilance, to guard and defend to the end of time the great charge he has committed to your keeping.[1]

The future of our nation depends heavily upon how well we as a nation remember the high cost of the freedom we must treasure. Each one of us must also sacrifice as we fight the subtle war that threatens our nation: the spiritual, economic, and political battles we face daily to maintain the often taken-for-granted freedoms we now enjoy.

The flag of the United States helps us remember the past and the sacrifices of men and women throughout the years. It flies as a symbol of our nation's unity and resolve to protect our freedoms in the present and the future.

As Christ-followers, we understand the importance of remembering, don't we? We read,

---

[1] President Andrew Jackson, "March 4, 1837 Farewell Address," University of Virginia Miller Center: https://millercenter.org/the-presidency/presidential-speeches/march-4-1837-farewell-address

study, memorize, contemplate, and meditate upon Scripture to remember. We celebrate the Sabbath on Sundays as a memorial to the resurrection of Christ and the freedom of sin His sacrifice gives us.

Another memorial is the Lord's Supper. The supper we read about in today's reading was a Passover meal. Jesus used the supper to teach His disciples about Himself as He applied the meaning of the meal to Himself.

"Do this in remembrance of Me," Jesus said in 1 Corinthians 11:24. We drink the wine and eat the bread as a way of remembering the life, ministry, and sacrifice of Christ (in the past). Through the supper, we express our praise and gratitude for the finished work of Christ on the cross and in His resurrection, and all that He has done and is doing for us as He delivers us from our sin.

By eating the Lord's Supper, through the Holy Spirit we are being nourished and empowered (in the present). The supper is a means of God's grace. Before we eat the supper, we are to examine ourselves so that we can eat it in a worthy manner (1 Corinthians 11:28-29).

Through the supper, our dedication to Christ

and His people is renewed in the present as we anticipate with hope His second coming (the future). Then with Him, we will partake in His kingdom (Matthew 25:29). Christ-followers must remember all that Christ has done for us in the past so that we are able to glorify Him through our lives in the present and future.

As an American, enjoy your Memorial Day celebrations, making certain you remember with thankfulness that these celebrations are possible because of those men and women who sacrificed their lives so that we could be free.

As a Christ-followers, may we ". . . exhort one another every day, as long as it is called 'today,' that none of [us] may be hardened by the deceitfulness of our sin" (Hebrews 3:13).

**Prayer:** Heavenly Father, thank You for the sacrifice of Your Son Jesus as He died, was buried, and rose again to purchase our freedom from the bondage of sin. Help us to obey Your commands and glorify You in and through everything we do and say. In Jesus' name, amen.

**Thought for the Day:** Our freedom in Christ was bought with Jesus' blood. Our freedom as Americans was bought with the blood of many men and women.

## Day 5: How Will I Be Remembered?

by Harriet
Read Jeremiah 9:23-24

*But let him who boasts boast in this, that he understands and knows me, that I am the LORD who practices steadfast love, justice and righteousness in the earth. . . .*
Jeremiah 9:24

This chapter has been about remembering, and in particular about remembering those who came before us, those we have lost, and those who have sacrificed so that we may enjoy the life we have. All of these thoughts of remembering others make me pause and think, how will I be remembered?

Have you ever pondered that? How will you be remembered when this life God has given to you to live is over?

When I was just twenty years old, a close friend of mine named Karen died very unexpectedly. She was murdered, actually, in a double murder that is still unsolved. I have mentioned her and this sad experience in my life in some of my other books and writings. For this devotion, I only want to recall something another friend of mine said at the time. A young man I was dating at the time who had also been a high school friend of Karen's mentioned a Bible verse to me as we were talking about her death and making plans to attend her funeral. He said, "Teach us to number our days, O Lord."

That verse is from Psalm 90:12 and in its entirety it says, "Teach us to number our days that we might apply our heart unto wisdom." Our days are numbered from the moment we are born. Psalm 139:16 tells us that all the days that God ordained for us to live were recorded in His book even before one came to be. What a sobering thought.

If I think about it, I have to ask myself, how do I want to be remembered? What great accomplishments do I want to be remembered for? These questions cause me to think of others I have known and what I remember most about them.

My father is in his nineties and, by God's grace, still alive. When I think back over his life, I am reminded that he had accomplishments that many will remember. He had a brilliant mind that he used to diagnose and prescribe medications and procedures that helped sick people get well in his medical practice. He had skillful hands with which he performed surgery. There are many who still comment to me how much my father meant to them and how he helped them. But that's not what I remember most about him. I remember his gentle smile, his tenderness, and the way he pursued knowledge, especially biblical knowledge.

One of my grandfathers was a poor, uneducated man. He did not have the accomplishments that this world applauds and holds in high esteem, but he was a hero to me. He stood six foot two inches tall with a strong body from working on a farm all of his life. He had a muscle in his arm he called his milking muscle—a small bulge close to his elbow that would pop up when he bent his arm and flexed his hands the way he would if he were milking a cow. In all of my life, I have never seen this small muscle so developed on anyone else. He said he formed it from a lifetime of milking a cow every day. Yet, what I remember most about my grandfather is the way his sky-blue eyes twinkled when he teased me, and how he squinted them in amusement, showing his laugh lines. I remember how his big hand engulfed mine when he held it while he said grace over meals, and how he struggled to read his Bible every day even though he only had a third-grade education.

The Bible tells us what is important in life. Micah 6:8 makes it pretty plain, "He has told you, O man, what is good, and what does the LORD require of you but to do justice, and to love kindness, and to walk humbly with your God?"

My days are numbered, just like everyone else. How do I want to be remembered? As someone who practiced justice, loved mercy, and walked humbly.

**Prayer:** Teach us to number our days, O Lord. Help us learn to apply our hearts to wisdom and to boast only in You. In Jesus' name, amen.

**Thought for the Day:** Let's strive to be someone whose life glorifies God such that when we are remembered, God will get the glory.

Chapter 2

# Blackberry Winter

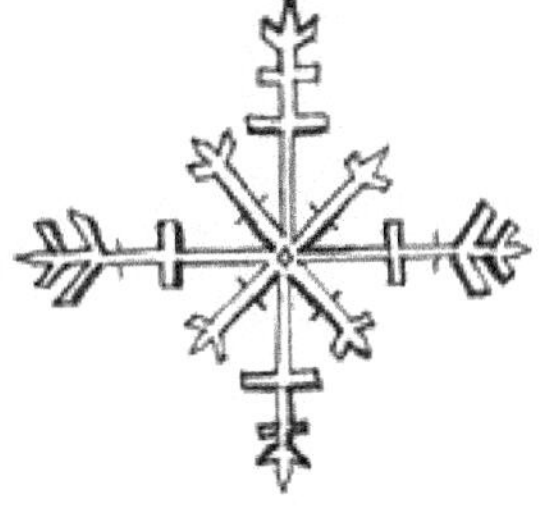

## Day 1: Blackberry Winter

by Harriet
Read Habakkuk 3:16-19

*Though the tree does not bud and*
*there are no grapes on the vines,*
*though the olive crop fails and the fields produce no food,*
*though there are no sheep in the pen*
*and no cattle in the stalls,*
*yet I will rejoice in the LORD,*
*I will be joyful in God my savior.*
*The Sovereign LORD is my strength. . . .*
Habakkuk 3:17-19a (NIV)

I first heard the term "Blackberry Winter" as a teenager living in West Virginia. I write a lot about my childhood in Africa because it made an indelible impression on me. But after the Biafran War broke out, my family returned to America and took up residence in a little mountain town in West Virginia where my father set up a medical practice. I spent my teenage years in the beautiful Appalachian Mountains; a far cry from Africa, but lovely in its own way.

Blackberry Winter is a colloquial expression

used in some rural parts of southern and midwestern America to refer to a cold snap that happens in late spring or early summer after crops have been planted and the fruit trees and bushes, like blackberries, have bloomed. Blackberry Winter is not a welcome season. Once people have put away their sweaters and coats and have high hopes for their fruit and vegetable crops, it comes unexpectedly, often with damaging consequences.

I'm a blackberry picker. I have scouted out rural areas near my house and know where blackberries grow wild. My heart leaps when I pass these spots in the early summer and see the bushes full of white blooms. I eagerly anticipate the buckets of blackberries I am going to pick in a few weeks. I can just taste the pies and cobblers I am going to make. When my children were small, I would roll the freshly-picked blackberries in sugar and freeze them. My children ate these straight from the freezer like candy. And each year, I hope we do not experience that dreaded thing known as Blackberry Winter. When it happens, I can cover my little garden plants, but I can't do anything about the wild blackberry bushes.

Where is God when things unexpectedly turn sour? How are we to respond when we are disappointed? The devotions in this chapter will focus on dealing with disappointment.

The prophet Habakkuk has profound things to say about how we are to act when we face disappointment. The disappointment Habakkuk experienced was way more than a few spoiled crops. Habakkuk 1:6 clues us in to his situation. He was a prophet and had received a vision in which God said that He was raising up the Chaldeans to come against the Jewish people. This was a wonder at the time because they had previously been allies. The Jewish people had learned to fear the Egyptians but not the Chaldeans. Yet, God showed Habakkuk that His plans included raising their friends up against them. Habakkuk knew what was coming and he trembled in fear, according to Habakkuk 3:16. Yet, what did he ultimately choose to do? He chose to praise God anyway and trust Him with his circumstances … and he expressed this trust in some of the most beautiful words in all of Scripture.

**Prayer:** Heavenly Father, You know all things. We

may be surprised by disappointments and sudden catastrophe, but nothing happens in our lives that is a surprise to You. Help us to follow Habakkuk's example and learn to trust You and praise You in all things. In Jesus' name, amen.

**Thought for the Day:** Blackberry Winters do not surprise God.

## Day 2: Warming a Cold Heart

by Shirley
Read Matthew 6:25-34

*Therefore, do not be anxious about tomorrow,*
*for tomorrow will be anxious for itself.*
*Sufficient for the day is its own trouble.*
Matthew 6:34

About this time of year I hear people say, "Summer is here," the weather is warmer and school is out. I absolutely love the brilliant colors on plants and the birds flitting around singing their joyful melodies. Some years it is hard to be sure that summer is here, since we often have a cold spell that comes in late spring when the blackberries are blooming, thus the name Blackberry Winter.

One late spring, I began seeing the signs of summer as the temperatures rose and the plants continued blooming and growing. My allergies were still in high gear, a small price to pay for enjoying the glorious beauty of God's magnificently colored creation. I expected

Blackberry Winter, but it never came.

One of my friends kept fretting over whether Blackberry Winter was going to kill some of her newly planted, delicate plants and their beautiful blooms. Each time I spoke with her, she would tell me the signs she saw that the fragile plants would be wiped out by a cold spell.

Blackberry Winter never came, and more and more plants burst into full bloom and grew into sturdy plants. In a few weeks, I asked this friend who had been fretting about a cold snap how all her newly planted plants were doing.

"I have fretted over them so much," she replied. "I didn't even take time to enjoy them and notice how they were growing."

In the same way my friend missed experiencing the beauty of her new plants, there are often things occurring in our lives that we do not fully experience and enjoy because we are so busy worrying about things. We allow our worry, expectation, and anticipation to block us from fully experiencing and enjoying the things that are happening around us. One friend fretted and grieved so much that her only child was going off to college that she didn't engage and enjoy spending time with her daughter before she left. Afterward, she not only missed and grieved for her daughter's presence, she regretted all the time she had spent fretting about her daughter's departure rather than spending time with her daughter while she was at home.

We are not even aware that our worry is stealing our joy, time, and energy. And we don't recognize that our worry does not take away any of the pain, struggles, or trials that will come our way in the future when the thing we are worrying about comes to pass.

There are other ways we miss experiencing things that are occurring all around us. Many single men and women put certain things on hold as they wait, hoping they will soon meet someone and get married.

We experience cold snaps in our spiritual lives, too. Suddenly we are aware that we are not experiencing the peace, joy, and strength that comes from a consistent walk with God. We get so busy fretting over what might happen that we allow the coldness to permeate our hearts and we do not live our lives in a way that honors God.

During these times, we often seek to warm our hearts by staying busy doing things or surrounding ourselves with lots of stuff. In time, we find out that our hearts are still as cold as they were and, in some instances, we find our hearts are even colder.

I heard Chuck Swindoll's program one day on the radio. He was telling the story of a plaque he had seen carved into the mantle of a fireplace that said, "If your heart is cold, my fire cannot warm it." He went on to talk about how a fireplace can warm your hands, feet, and body, but not your heart, because only "the fire of the living God" can warm a heart.

God's fire burns eternally and never cools down; that is why God's fire can warm our hearts.

**Prayer:** Heavenly Father, help us to stop the cold snaps in our lives from permeating our hearts. May we be filled with Your fire that truly warms our hearts so we will trust in You and share the warmth of Your mercy, grace, and love with others. In Jesus' name, amen.

**Thought for the Day:** Only the fire of the living God can warm your heart—not people, things, nor circumstances.

## Day 3: By the Rivers of Babylon

by Harriet
Read Psalm 137:1-4

*By the rivers of Babylon we sat*
*and wept when we remembered Zion.*
Psalm 137:1 (NIV)

Many of the disappointments we read about in the Bible are much worse than just a cold snap that causes a crop failure. These disappointments and devastations in the Bible happen to God's people. I don't buy into a prosperity gospel that teaches that following Christ will always bring success, good health, and abundance in every area of life. There are too many places in Scripture where things did not go well for God's people for me to conclude that a prosperity gospel is valid. Today's passage is one of those places.

The poignant words in this psalm tell a sad story. The Jewish people had been taken into captivity, and in this passage their captors are mocking them. When they were asked to sing songs of Zion, it was not a sincere request—it was a mockery of all the Jewish people valued and believed in. Does this still happen today? We are not taken into captivity in America, but that does still happen in other countries. And even here in the US, we are often mocked for the things we believe in and value.

It's interesting to note that the captured Hebrews in this passage did not weep about how they were being treated or the fact that they had been taken into captivity. Those things made them angry, as can be seen later in the passage. What caused them to weep was their memory of Zion—the destruction of their temple and the dismantling of their worship places and practices. The songs they were asked to sing in a mocking way were songs of worship. Their captors were mocking their God, Yahweh Himself.

I am reminded of places around the globe where churches are being burned down and Christians are suffering persecution. For the most part, we have been spared that in America. We still have a land where we are free to worship God. That is a right we need to work diligently to keep and never take for granted. Though we still live in freedom here, the sad scene described in these verses is still played out in many places all over the world.

I am reminded of another passage. In 1 Kings 18 we find the story in which Elijah called down fire from heaven even when 450 prophets of Baal could not. A few years ago, I had a Sunday school teacher explain something about this passage that I did not know. In Elijah's day, different gods were worshiped in different territories. The land where the miracle occurred was Baal's territory, not Yahweh's territory. If this miracle had occurred in Yahweh's territory, it would not have seemed quite as amazing to the people. The thing that made it an even greater miracle in their eyes was that it happened in Baal's territory. Yahweh could bring about the miracle, while Baal remained powerless to do so. It meant that even in Baal's territory, Yahweh ruled.

Then my Sunday school teacher said something that I will never forget. He said, "God is still God, even in Baal's territory!"

Yes, God is still God, no matter the place or the circumstances. He was still with His people when they sat by the rivers of Babylon weeping, and He is still with the persecuted church today. Psalm 34:18 reassures us that He is near to the brokenhearted, and He is near to us regardless of the difficult or inconvenient things that confront us.

**Prayer:** Father, You are gracious to us, drawing near to us in our time of need. May we set our eyes on You and not on our circumstances. Hold us close, heal us in the places we need healing, and lead us out to the place where You would have us to be. In Jesus' name, amen.

**Thought for the Day:** God is still God even, or especially, when we are facing difficult days.

# Day 4: Earmuffs and Gloves (a.k.a. Flexibility)

by Shirley
Read Matthew 2:1-12

*And being warned in a dream not to return to Herod, they departed to their own country by another way.*
Matthew 2:12

One early spring when I lived in the greater metro Washington, D.C., area, my friends and I decided to go down to McLean, Virginia, to Great Falls Park, and have a picnic. The weather leading up to our Saturday picnic was gorgeous. It was sunshiny with a nice breeze. Each of us was to bring certain things we would need for our picnic, like food, drinks, blankets, and trash bags. We were all excited about our first spring outing for the season.

When I woke up early Saturday morning, I jumped into the shower, had my quiet time, and turned on the news while I fixed and ate breakfast.

What had the news reporter said? Certainly I hadn't heard her correctly. A cold snap had settled in the night before, and the high for the day was only supposed to be thirty degrees. Oh wait, they were expecting it to be a much warmer thirty-three degrees in McLean.

Before long my phone rang and a friend said, “Did you hear the weather? We can’t go on a picnic when it’s freezing cold.” She wanted to call off the picnic and gather at one of our homes and have an indoor picnic. Since she was the one who was organizing the picnic, I told her that I would love to go to Great Falls Park as planned, but that she could poll the others and decide what we would do.

Most did not want to picnic in the freezing weather. Three of us wanted to go to Great Falls for an adventure. The guy who called me with the results said, “Grab your coat, earmuffs, gloves, and some heavy blankets, we’re going to a picnic.”

I didn’t have earmuffs and my gloves were made to make a fashion statement more than to keep hands warm, so the other two brought along extras and shared with me.

We got to Great Falls Park and walked around exploring for a while. We didn’t have to worry if the food would spoil because it would be kept very cold while it was in the car.

When it came time to eat, the deviled eggs were a little frozen and the cold wind was whipping around us, but we enjoyed every delicious bite of our food, and since there were supposed to be more folks with us, we had food to share with several other people who had braved the cold to spend time at the park.

We had to do a few things a little differently from what we had planned, like bundle up with so much clothing that we could barely move and take a bite of something and cover our heads with a blanket while we chewed our food. We laughed and had a great time getting to know those who joined us.

Okay, having a picnic in freezing weather while bundled up so we don't freeze doesn't sound like fun to most people. For the three of us, it was a story to retell and enjoy often. We had some great adventures that space won't allow me to tell here.

The friends who stayed back and had an indoor picnic couldn't believe all the things we did and how much fun we seemed to have in spite of the cold. I understand them wanting to stay warm and they were flexible, just in a different way from the rest of us.

Had we not gone that day, I might have never met a woman with whom I am still in contact. We have laughed, cried, and prayed together for the many years since that picnic.

I credit growing up on the mission field for teaching me to be flexible and not let the little things change my plans. Of course, freezing cold weather was not what we faced in Nigeria, but we did face dry season, rainy season, washed out roads, all kinds of creatures, and other things that threatened to deter the missionaries from their mission.

This story is a great reminder that we are to be flexible and ready for whatever the Lord brings across our paths. In counseling, I often counsel with women who want to be in control of every little portion of every situation. If things don't go the way they planned, they become angry, sad, gloomy, and downright pitiful.

The Lord constantly leads or places us in places and situations that give us opportunities to be flexible. In addition, when we prayerfully step out in faith to be flexible, He gives us the grace, mercy, and strength to endure and to finish well. We learn to give up the illusion that we are in control and invite God to be in control.

Today's passage is the account of the wise men looking for Jesus—the Messiah. Herod told them to come back and report to him when they found the baby. Instead, the wise men followed the Lord's prompting to go back home another way. Had they not been flexible and willing to go a different route, Herod would have had opportunity to find and maybe even kill Jesus. The next time something doesn't go the way you planned it, pray, asking God to help you be flexible and trust His leadership.

**Prayer:** Heavenly Father, help us learn to be flexible and to trust in Your grace, mercy, and strength to lead us in whatever we do and wherever we go. In Jesus' name, amen.

**Thought for the Day:** God uses our flexibility in situations to strengthen and stretch our faith in Him and to teach us to depend upon Him more.

## Day 5: Praise the Lord, Anyway!

by Harriet
Read Philippians 4:4-7

*Rejoice in the LORD always. I will say it again; Rejoice!*
Philippians 4:4 (NIV)

"PTLA!"

I've heard this expression all of my life. It stands for "Praise the Lord anyway." Though a valid concept, it is often used lightly and said when something not-so-awful occurs. Christians tend to throw this line around during the Blackberry Winters of their lives when nothing more has happened than the inconvenience of having to cover their crops or pull out the sweaters they had packed away. Yet, it would be good to remember this and practice it even in the worst of times because we can. We serve a God who is mighty and powerful. He can change our circumstances, overcome the obstacles in our lives that threaten to block us, or help us walk through the difficult things we may face. God is with us always and worthy to be praised.

When one of my sons was little, he had a picture book that told the story of Jonah. He enjoyed the pictures of the whale and Jonah in its belly, but one night I saw him staring at the picture of Jonah hiding in the lower level of a ship, behind a barrel. I sat down beside my son. He pointed to the picture and said, "Jonah was hiding from God." From there the conversation went something like this:

Me: "Yeah, but you can't hide from God, can you?"

My son: "Yes, you can."

Me: "No, you can't. That is the whole point of the story. You can't hide from God. Here, let me read the story to you again."

But he kept insisting a person could hide from God. The more I said that was not possible, the more he insisted it was. I grew a bit exasperated and stated rather emphatically, "No you can't. You can't hide from God."

This prompted my son to reply, "Mommy, you *can* hide from God. You can." But then he added,

"But . . . God can always find you."

That's such good news. Jonah may not have thought the fact that God could find him was good news when he hid from God in the bottom of the boat. Later, however, when he found himself swallowed up by a giant fish, still alive in the fish's belly, most likely feeling his skin burning from the fish's gastric juices, and facing certain death, he cried out to God in desperation, and then he learned just how wonderful a truth it is that God can always find us.

God knows what we are dealing with in our lives. Maybe you are in a season of joy and a time of personal success. Or maybe you are experiencing a challenging time when your plans have suddenly been ruined or altered. Whether we are living a life that pleases Him or, like Jonah, are trying to run away and hide from Him, God knows us, and He loves us. His ways are not our ways, but His ways are always perfect, and He can be trusted. That is the reason we can and should praise Him anyway, regardless of the Blackberry Winters in our lives.

**Prayer:** Heavenly Father, You are a mighty God.

You never leave us or forsake us. You have ways that we do not understand, but they are perfect. Teach our hearts to trust You. Grant us a greater measure of faith. Teach us to praise You regardless of our circumstances. In Jesus' name, amen.

**Thought for the Day:** We truly can praise God anyway.

## Chapter 3

# *Lazy Days of Summer*

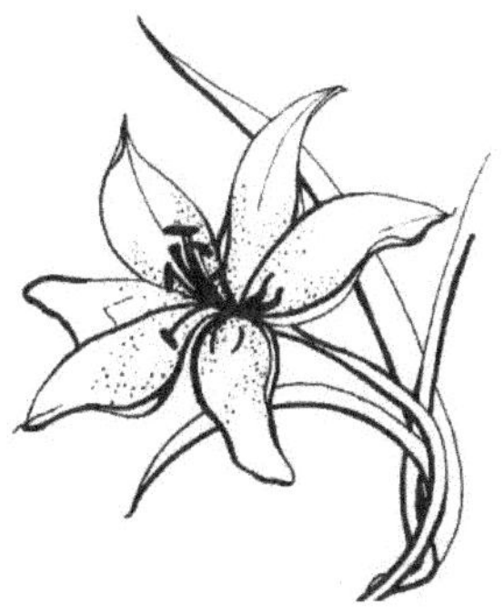

## Day 1: A Father, Dad, Daddy

by Shirley
Read Hebrews 12:5-11

*Only take care, and keep your soul diligently,*
*lest you forget the things that your eyes have seen,*
*and lest they depart from your heart all the days of your life.*
*Make them known to your children*
*and your children's children.*
Deuteronomy 4:9

Most people called him Ray. I called him Father, Dad, and my daddy. All four of these point to the same man.

"Father is a formal title for 'a male parent' or 'someone who has begotten a child,'" according to Merriam-Webster. When I refer to Ray with this title, I am referring to his parental, authoritative, and disciplinary role in my life.

When my father told me to do something, I was to do it immediately, joyfully, and completely, or there would be consequences—a.k.a. discipline.

I remember one time when my mom left to go grocery shopping that my father told me I could not go play with my friend until I cleaned up my room and put the dishes in the dishwasher. He immediately left to visit someone in the hospital, which I, of course, took as my cue to go play with my friend. After some time had passed, I heard my father calling me.

I was grounded, which meant I could not play with any friends, and for a whole week I was to do a ton of chores. I could, of course, go to church services.

"Dad" is a more informal title. A handwritten note in a file I have on fathering reads, "Being a dad means 'being there' for your child(ren)." When I refer to my dad, I am referring to the man who took care of his family, protected us, discussed—yes, even argued—theology with me, and whose advice was always solid.

I began referring to Ray as Dad in my teen years. It is more informal and indicative of me becoming more independent of my parents, of my becoming more mature—okay, maybe older is more accurate.

One Saturday night when I was in high school, friends invited me to go to a movie. Dad gave me permission to go as long as I came home right after the movie.

The group decided we should go get something to eat after the movie, and I didn't want to miss out on anything. I did have a dime (remember, this was the olden days when there were no cell phones) and could have called and let my friends help me convince Dad to let me go get something to eat, but alas. . . .

When I walked in the house, there sat Dad. I could tell immediately that I was in big trouble. He didn't even look angry; he was just sitting there looking at me. Dad said, "Sweetheart …" and inhaled deeply. He did not raise his voice; in fact, he spoke in that measured and controlled tone of voice that indicated my social life had ended—forever. Mom joined us at the table.

Dad reminded me how I continually told him that I was old enough to have more freedom, to make decisions on my own, and that I knew what was right and wrong. Yep, of one thing I was certain—no more social life for me.

We spent the next hour or so making sure that I knew how the Bible—and Dad and Mom—

defined right and wrong. I learned about forgiveness for sinning against God and disobeying my parents. And, I learned there are consequences to sin.

All these decades later, I remember that discussion almost word-for-word. I learned God's definition of right and wrong, although many of my actions since then have shown that I didn't really understand; for if I did, I would have made much different choices in a myriad of situations.

"Daddy is a title for 'a person's father—used especially by young children.'" (Merriam-Webster)

When I was a child and even up into my early thirties when he died, I called Ray Daddy. Now, when I speak of certain memories, or I am really missing him, "Daddy" is what comes to mind.

I was seven or eight years old when I took it upon myself to get something unplugged from an electrical outlet in the wall. I do not remember what it was, but it would not come out. Being a brilliant youngster, I went into the kitchen, got a knife. . . .

The shock knocked the breath out of me as I landed on my rear end, and it scared me. When I screamed bloody murder, my Daddy, Mommy, and brother Tim came running. Before he even got to me, Daddy saw the knife on the floor near the outlet and realized what had happened. Daddy scooped me up into his arms. He and Mommy checked my hands for burns and asked me questions so they could determine if I had fried my brain.

Meanwhile, Daddy was holding me tightly, while whispering—well, actually, he wasn't whispering because I wouldn't have heard him over my screams—comforting words: "Daddy's got you. You're going to be all right. Shhhh. Mommy and Daddy are here."

They declared me to be all right after a visit to the emergency room, then my Daddy carefully and tenderly ensured I understood what happened so I wouldn't repeat it.

Thinking about all of this brought today's passage to mind: "And have you completely forgotten this word of encouragement that addresses you as a father addresses his son?"

I am all too often reminded of the lessons I learned through the comfort, protection, and instruction I received from my father. Remembering my father, dad, and daddy, always evokes myriad emotions and sometimes leaves me feeling very unprotected and alone.

Yet, in His grace, the Lord always reminds me of several things. I have a Heavenly Father, who forgave my sin and saved me from an eternity of punishment through His wrath. This same Father God (Dad) created me to live in intimate relationship with Him as I read, study, meditate upon, memorize, and listen to preaching of the Holy Spirit-inspired word, and through prayer. This same Abba Father lovingly and protectively holds me securely in the grip of his grace.

While Ray Crowder was far from perfect, I am blessed to have had an earthly father, dad, and daddy, from whom I learned about my Heavenly Father, Savior, Lord, and Comforter.

It is likely that some of you did not have an earthly father who honored God that may make reading this difficult. Remember, Your Heavenly Father loves you and is always with you.

**Prayer:** Heavenly Father, thank You for our earthly fathers who love You and us as they teach us Your commands and how to be obedient to Your word. For those who did not, or do not, have fathers who know You, I pray You will bring godly men into their lives who can help give them a glimpse of You as their Heavenly Father. In Jesus' name. amen.

**Thought for the Day:** Your Heavenly Father loves you as He protects, comforts, provides for, and disciplines you.

## Day 2: My Father's Arms

by Harriet
Read Deuteronomy 33:26-27

*The eternal God is your dwelling place,*
*and underneath are the everlasting arms. . . .*
Deuteronomy 33:27

My father taught me to swim by having me jump from the side of the pool into his open arms while he waited in the water to catch me. We didn't have a swimming pool in Ogbomoso, the Nigerian city where I grew up, but there was a pool in Ibadan, a larger city a couple of hours away by car. Being a larger city, Ibadan offered stores we also did not have in Ogbomoso, so once a month, my family piled into our car and made a day trip to Ibadan. Often, my dad took us kids to the pool for at least several hours during the day. Sometimes, my mom dropped us off and we swam while she shopped, and other times she swam with us if there wasn't as much shopping to be done that month. This Ibadan pool was where I learned not to be afraid of the water by jumping into my father's arms. He never dropped me, and never did I hesitate to jump to him. I felt secure in my father's arms. As time went by, he encouraged me to jump directly into the water while he waited close by. I always knew he would not let me drown.

When I became an adult, I still knew I could call on my father for help. I recall a time the brakes in my car failed. I was driving down a hill with my children in the car. The car in front of me stopped at a light at the bottom of the hill. I applied my brakes, but they didn't work. The road I traveled had a steep ditch on my right, so I steered into the left lane to swerve around the stopped car. Fortunately, there was no oncoming traffic in the left lane. After safely swerving past the car, I allowed my car to slow down on its own to around 20 miles per hour and was thus able to make it home safely.

At that time in my life, my husband and I had no means with which to buy new brakes, so reluctantly, I called my father. I apologized for having to ask to borrow money, telling him that we had considered all other options and had exhausted all of our resources. My sweet father replied, "Honey, until you have called me, you have never exhausted all of your resources."

Every year, Father's Day falls on a Sunday in June, just as summer's lazy days are starting to get into full swing. And every year, I recall again how blessed I have been to have had the father I had. He's been a wonderful earthly father. His arms have caught me many times in my life, whether literally or symbolically, whether it was his outstretched arms of financial help, or even spiritual help.

As wonderful as my earthly father has been, my Heavenly Father is even more wonderful. He rides the heavens to be our help, according to verse 26 of this passage. And He, too, stretches out his arms to catch us with his everlasting arms.

**Prayer:** Thank You Lord for Your word that helps us to understand You better. Thank You for Your everlasting arms that support us when we need it and catch us when we fall. In Jesus' name, amen.

**Thought for the Day:** God rides the heavens to be our help. He is a dwelling place and underneath are the everlasting arms. What a beautiful picture those words paint.

## Day 3: The Good Ol' Summertime

by Shirley
Read 1 Thessalonians 2:1-13

*Because we loved you so much,*
*we were delighted to share with you*
*not only the gospel of God but our lives as well.*
1 Thessalonians 2:8b (NIV)

Today, summers are not much different for me than other seasons, except for the weather changes and different clothing, but when I was a child, summers were very different. I have such wonderful childhood memories of summertime in Nigeria and America. In Nigeria, our summers were filled with fun games, swimming, climbing trees, visiting missionary families at other mission stations, and having them visit us. In America, we took trips to the mountains and beaches, visited family and Nigeria Mission family, spent time at youth camps, and went on short-term missions. My friends and I rode our bicycles all over town. We went to drive-in movies, church picnics and cookouts, and spent days at the lake, swimming and fishing. Dad did a lot of barbecuing. He spent days making his special marinade and barbecue sauce, then would stand at the grill for hours cooking the ribs and chicken. Everyone who joined us would bring one or two of their specialty foods and everyone would enjoy a feast that usually ended with Mom's homemade custard ice cream. I would help Mom can a lot of fruit and vegetables and help Dad work in the garden or yard.

Catching fireflies was something we did on both continents. What fun to catch the fireflies, put them in a jar or container with breathing holes punched in it, and watch the fireflies light up. I'm still fascinated by fireflies. Our time spent staying with Grandmother and various aunts and uncles was always filled with adventures. Summer seemed to allow more time for us to be with our church family—not just the children my age, but whole families together.

As I look back, I realize how hard my parents worked to enable us to have those fun-filled days of summer. Their schedules didn't change much, except that the amount of time they spent hauling us around from place to place increased exponentially.

Our vacation trips were filled with stops along the way at flea markets, junk stores, historical landmarks, and wonderful scenic views, and often, these trips included pulling into a parking area, hiking down to a mountain stream and wading in the cool, refreshing water. My childhood summers were fun-filled and carefree days, with the exception of the few chores for which I was responsible.

While there were many things we did during our summers—many which left indelible marks in my memory—what I remember most about our summers is people. We got to see family, Nigeria Mission family, and old friends of Mom and Dad. We also met new people wherever we went.

What made these summers so special wasn't all the experiences we had, things we did, nor places we went, it was the people with whom we shared those things and places, many with whom we shared a common bond in Christ.

In today's passage, the Apostle Paul tells the Thessalonians that the sacrifices he made and the hardships he experienced while ministering to them weren't a burden for him; that he was "well pleased" to minister to them. He also tells them he is "affectionately desirous" or "affectionately longing," as the King James Version puts it, for them because the Thessalonians had become so dear to him. Paul is saying he was a spiritual father to them, feeding them God's word, and even risking his own life for them to hear and learn God's word.

Paul was also encouraging them to continue living holy lives, according to the things he had taught them. He was giving them comfort and assurance that Christ would come again for them.

To say that is what was happening with the people with whom we interacted over the summer is a stretch in some ways. However, as we interacted with each other, we and they were encouraged to continue walking in the faith and living lives that glorified God, and we were comforted and reassured by the reminders that Christ is coming again.

Are your summers filled with people who encourage you to continue living lives that glorify

God and who comfort and reassure you with reminders that Christ is coming again?

**Prayer:** Heavenly Father, thank You for those whom You put in our path who encourage us to continue living holy lives and give us comfort and assurance of Your return. In Jesus' name. amen.

**Thought for the Day:** Look for those whom God will bring across your path so that you may encourage to continue living lives that glorify and please Him.

## Day 4: Do You Hear the Whistle?

by Harriet
Read Zechariah 10:7-8, John 10:3-4

*I will whistle for them to gather them together,*
*for I have redeemed them. . . .*
Zechariah 10:8 (NASB)

Years ago, when my husband, John, and I were a young married couple with a growing family, he used to enjoy playing on our church's softball team in the local church league. We are older now and these days, after getting several artificial joints, he has replaced recreational games like church-league softball and basketball with occasional golf outings. But back then he loved to play on the church team. John was a three-sport athlete in high school, playing soccer, basketball, and baseball. I never played sports—though I did manage to make the cheerleading squad—but once married, I never participated in women's leagues the way my husband participated in the men's leagues. We always made his church ball games a family event, though. My three children loved accompanying their father to his games—not because they took pleasure in watching their dad play, but because the land behind the church where the softball fields were located had wide-open green space where they could run and play. I would sit in the stands with the other wives while our children played in that open field nearby.

This made a perfect set-up because, though the children felt as if they were running free, we mothers could see every one of them from our seats in the stands. It was a good distance away, though, and if some child fell or skinned his or her knee, we had a pretty long hike to get to them, but at least we could see every move they made.

When the ball game ended, the time would come to gather the children for the trip home. And although we could see the children off in the distance, they could not hear us if we called to them. Usually they didn't see us waving our arms, either, because they were too preoccupied with their play. They could hear my husband's shrill whistle, though, so he would whistle for them when it was time to stop playing and go home. I could see their little heads turning in our direction when they heard their father's whistle, and I would stand and wave them in. This routine became familiar to them and they would always know it was time to go home when they heard their father's whistle.

The Old Testament book of Zechariah tells of a time when God will whistle for His children to come to Him. When I read this passage a few years ago, the memory of my husband whistling for our children flashed through my mind. It's easy for me to imagine the scenario being like those days of my husband's summer softball games. Like my children, we will recognize our Father's whistle and respond. I picture it to be sort of like those special dog whistles which only dogs can hear. When God whistles, His children will hear even as the unbelieving world goes about with their lives, unaware of God's call.

John 10:3-4 says that God calls his sheep and they follow Him because they know His voice. Is God's voice calling you today? Is He whistling for you? Do you recognize His voice in your life? What is He asking you to do?

**Prayer:** Heavenly Father, make us to hear Your voice when You call. Lead us to the places You would have us go. Whistle for us today. In Jesus' name, amen.

**Thought for the Day:** Do you hear God's whistle?

# Day 5: Don't Waste Those Lazy Days

by Shirley

Read Psalm 15

*He who walks blamelessly and does what is right and speaks truth in his heart . . . shall never be moved.*
Psalm 15:2, 5b

I love summer—except for the heat. I have heard all my life about the lazy days of summer, although at times as a child and even now as an adult I can't quite grasp that concept. Many people say there is a slower pace in the summer, but I'm not so sure about that either. Are you?

It is true that the schedule opens up when school is out, but those with children or grandchildren know that in the summer those school hours are filled with a gazillion activities that require parents and grandparents to get the children from one activity to the next. There are always fun things to do such as going to the zoo, botanical gardens, or the lake, having a cookout or picnic, or going to an outdoor concert or event, and having leisurely visits with family and friends. Christ-followers often have Vacation Bible School, church picnics and camps, and choir retreats.

As an adult, my summer schedule is fairly regular; although it seems slower, I'm actually very busy. I work a regular schedule at my job, I have responsibilities at my church on Sundays and Wednesday evenings, and at the time of this writing, Thursday evenings for a Bible study I'm teaching. The balance of my time at night and my days off, I write, edit for others, work on getting blog posts ready, do a great deal of biblical counseling, and whatever else the Lord lays before me. In the summer, I have a fairly heavy schedule of speaking engagements and conferences to attend, making June and July very busy months for me.

It is easy for me to get so involved in all the ministry, writing, and working, as well as having fun and "taking it easy" that some of my routines get disrupted. Sadly, I get lazy in my time with the Lord in communicating with God through prayer and Bible reading, studying, memorizing, contemplating, and meditating, and allow my time with the Lord to get squeezed out by all that I'm doing.

Not that these ministry, work, and fun things are sinful in and of themselves, but when I give them a higher priority than my time with the Lord or do not use them as opportunities to worship God, my priorities become sinful.

You would think that someone who works with two churches, teaches Sunday school and Bible studies, writes devotionals, and speaks at Christian conferences, retreats, and seminars would do a lot of praying and spending time in the Bible preparing for all these things. Well, I do; knowing the Lord will help me glean biblical truth to set forth in my writing or teaching.

The danger for me, and maybe for you, is going on "autopilot" by relying on what I already know and not looking at the Scripture afresh to see what the Holy Spirit would lead me to learn or to understand an application I had not known before.

We know that all of life is worship—and that's where we often get into trouble. We worship all the things we are doing—ministry, work, or fun—

instead of making everything we do acts of worship of God.

My friend Dr. Howard Eyrich speaks about it this way,

> … getting your ticket punched, so to speak, by having a twenty-minute devotional time is insufficient. Quiet time, outside the context of worshipful living, will likely only salve one's conscience … abide in Christ so that your life will look like the life depicted in Psalm 15.[2]

Psalm 1 tells us to meditate upon God's word all the time. When we are immersed in prayer and the Bible, we will have the strength to accomplish all the things the Lord places before us, and to rely upon Him for rest and strength. Then we can do as the Apostle Paul, in 1 Corinthians 15:58, reminds us that we are to do. In the midst of our busy and

---

[2] "Hope for New Beginnings" by Howard Eyrich & Shirley Crowder, Growth Advantage Communications, 2019, page 13.

lazy summers, let's not forget to abide in Christ as we worship Him in and through all that we do.

**Prayer:** Heavenly Father, thank You for the beauty of Your creation that we can enjoy during summer. Forgive us for allowing our busyness to squeeze You out of our schedules and lives. Give us a passion to know You better. In Jesus' name, amen.

**Thought for the Day:** Spend time with God in prayer and Bible reading, studying, memorizing, and meditating on Scripture.

Chapter 4

# Summer Hymns

## Day 1: There is Sunlight on the Hilltop

by Shirley
Read 2 Corinthians 4:1-6

*For God who said, "Let light shine out of darkness" has shone in our hearts to give the light of the knowledge of the glory of God in the face of Jesus Christ.*
2 Corinthians 4:6

A group of friends talked me into going cave exploring when I was in my thirties. The two men and the lady were experienced cavers. Me? Not so much.

They picked me up and I was wearing the type of clothing and shoes I had been instructed to wear. They provided me with all the equipment I would need for our adventure. I knew there would be times I would not know what to do, but knew I was with three experienced cavers.

It was a beautiful bright, sunshiny day as we began our cave exploring. I was third in line behind the lead man and the lady. For the first bit of our adventure into the cave, the sunshine provided light so that we could see where we were stepping, and I could examine all the things to which they were drawing my attention.

It surprised me that I began to see crickets, because those around me were not making any sounds. My friends explained that cave-crickets usually don't make sounds when light is present, but if there were no light we would likely hear them chirping. One of the men said that once we got deeper into the cave where the sunlight didn't reach, we could turn our lights out and listen for their chirps.

Soon, all the natural light from the sun disappeared and our way was lit by the lights we carried with us. We climbed down into a tunnel to see what we would find. It was then that I remembered we wanted to turn out all our lights and listen to the crickets chirp. The other three sat on the cave floor, but I was afraid of spiders and other things crawling over me, so I decided to stand. I was instructed to turn out my lights first. Then, we waited a few minutes and the next person's lights were turned out.

After another few minutes the lady said, "Are you ready to experience real darkness?"

I heartily said, "Yes."

Suddenly we were surrounded by a darkness I had never experienced before. The darkness came on so suddenly I lost my sense of balance and started falling forward. Thankfully, as I screamed the man right beside me reached out to grab me and broke my fall in the process.

By the time he helped me sit down on the cave floor, I was badly shaken, my heart was beating a gazillion beats a minute, and my breathing was labored. They asked if I was hurt and I told them no, that it just scared me. I told them I was fine staying in the dark and listening for the chirping crickets—by that time I was sure I had scared all of them off by my scream.

It didn't take but a few more seconds for me to announce that we needed to turn on the lights quickly. I was a bit surprised when I heard the click of a lighter. That tiny flame was so bright against the darkness of the cave and I began to calm down.

At just about the same time, two of us said, "Wow! That's like God's light." The lady with us began quoting today's key passage, "For God who said, 'Let light shine out of darkness' has shone in our hearts to give the light of the knowledge of the glory of God in the face of Jesus Christ."

The statement in 1 John 1:5 came to mind and I quoted, "This is the message we have heard from him and proclaim to you, that God is light, and in him is no darkness at all."

We decided we probably needed to head for the entrance. One of the guys said, "My grandmother used to sing a hymn about sunlight. I don't remember the tune, but the words were something about the beautiful sunlight in my heart and how Jesus' smile banishes sadness."

It was a fun adventure, but I'm not sure I'll be doing that type of caving again. I went home and journaled about this adventure and wrote the words he said so I could remember them. I also made a note, "That little flicker from a light was able to chase away the chaos—at least in my mind—of the darkness and calm me down. And guess what, the light of God shines brighter and more brilliantly into our lives."

I hadn't thought about caving again until I

began studying for these summer devotionals. I found the journal entry and was able to find the hymn to which my friend was referring while we were in the cave.

It is the hymn, *There is Sunlight on the Hilltop*, by Mrs. M. T. Haughey. The refrain is a little different from what my friend quoted, but I love it.

> Oh, the sunlight! Beautiful sunlight!
> Oh, the sunlight in the heart!
> Jesus' smile can banish sadness;
> It is sunlight in the heart.

The hymn is based on today's passage from 2 Corinthians that talks about the light of God shining in our hearts giving "the light of the knowledge of the glory of God in the face of Jesus Christ."

Let's look at the stanzas of this hymn:

> It is sunlight in the heart.
> There is sunlight on the hilltop,
> There is sunlight on the sea;
> And the golden beams are sleeping
> On the soft and verdant lea;

But a richer light is filling
All the chambers of my heart;
For Thou dwellest there, my Savior
And 'tis sunlight where Thou art.

In the dust I leave my sadness,
As the garb of other days,
For Thou robest me with gladness,
And Thou fillest me with praise;
And to that bright home of glory
Which Thy love hath won for me,
In my heart and mind ascending,
My glad spirit follows Thee.

Loving Savior, Thou hast bought me,
And my life, my all, is Thine;
Let the lamp Thy love hath lighted
To Thy praise and glory shine;
And to that bright home of glory
Which Thy love hath won for me,
In my heart and mind ascending,
My glad spirit follows Thee.

A handwritten note in my Bible beside this

passage says, "Satan attempts to hide people from the light that streams from the gospel in our hearts and minds that reveals God's glory in Christ." We respond to seeing God's glory by believing.

Through God's mercy and grace, we come to a saving knowledge of God. We are transformed by the Holy Spirit and given "the light of the knowledge of the glory of God in the face of Jesus Christ" so we can see.

**Prayer:** Heavenly Father, thank You for the light that came into our darkened hearts that shone through Your word. Take away any sin that would keep us from seeing Your glory. May we continue being transformed into Your image. In Jesus' name, amen.

**Thought for the Day:** A light richer than the sunlight on the hilltop fills the heart of Christ-followers because our Savior dwells within us.

## Day 2: As Pants the Hart for Cooling Streams

by Shirley
Read Psalm 42

*As the deer pants for flowing streams,*
*so pants my soul for you.*
*My soul thirsts for God, for the living God.*
Psalm 42:1

A friend and I were exploring the woods in Northern Virginia on a hot and humid summer afternoon. An hour or so into our hike, we stopped to rest in the shade under some trees. I was worn out and ready to head back to the comfort of the air-conditioned car. There was a guy hiking from the opposite direction who stopped to rest under the same trees. We began chatting with him and learned that just about a half mile ahead of us we would find a wonderful, cool, clean, stream. He described the beautiful scene, and of course, we couldn't miss seeing it.

We had hiked what seemed to be about five

miles—it was actually about a half mile—and I was very hot and tired and ready to give up our quest to find the stream and go back to the car. My friend dropped his backpack and started climbing up a tree to get a view of our surroundings. He started talking about how beautiful it was, but said all he could see were trees. I climbed up into the tree so I could see what he was talking about. He jumped out of the tree to grab his camera, then climbed back up the tree to take pictures, including one of me sitting on a tree branch. He handed me the camera so I could take a picture of him sitting on a branch just below me. It was then that I saw a beautiful stag. We snapped some pictures and watched him amble off in the direction we were heading.

I thought the stag was certainly heading for the stream, and that if we followed him from a safe distance back, we wouldn't spook him, and he would lead us to the stream.

After a few minutes, I began to hear the babbling stream ahead of us. We stayed behind in the trees and bushes while the stag crossed over to drink from the stream. After drinking the refreshing water, the stag wandered away.

As we stepped out from behind the trees, a couple of squirrels that had been playing in the stream scampered up a tree to find safety. We sat at the edge of the stream and took off our socks and shoes and waded into the stream. The water was very cold and crystal clear. It felt so good. We were immediately refreshed and invigorated.

As we sat and waited for our feet to dry, we soaked up the sun and the beauty that surrounded us—trees of different varieties and beautiful wildflowers. Birds were flitting around and playing a little downstream from us.

Nathan Tate and Nicholas Brady wrote the lyrics of a beautiful hymn, *As Pants the Hart for Cooling Streams* (a hart is a deer).

This hymn is based on today's key passage. While it is not sinful to want relief from the circumstances we face, we must recognize that just as we need water to live, the need for God in our lives is even greater than our need for water. This hymn beautifully expresses the Psalmist's deepest, strongest, and most sincere thirst, or desire, for God alone.

Many of our lives are parched and dried up

because we have sought things that have deterred us from pursuing God. Instead of coming to church to worship God and be taught the truth of God's word, we often come to church to be spoon- and bottle-fed things that will make us feel better about ourselves, and we begin to dry out.

The Psalmist and the hymn writer tell us how we can avoid becoming parched and dried out. We must "pant" or pursue God so that we experience the nourishment of our soul through His presence.

> As pants the hart for cooling streams
> When heated in the chase,
> So longs my soul, O God, for Thee,
> And Thy refreshing grace.
>
> Why restless, why cast down, my soul?
> Trust God, who will employ
> His aid for thee, and change these sighs
> To thankful hymns of joy.
>
> For Thee, my God, the living God,
> My thirsty soul doth pine
> Oh, when shall I behold Thy face,

Thou Majesty Divine?

God of my strength, how long shall I,
Like one forgotten, mourn,
Forlorn, forsaken, and exposed
To my oppressor's scorn?

Why restless, why cast down, my soul?
Hope still, and thou shalt sing
The praise of Him who is thy God,
Thy health's eternal spring.

**Prayer:** Heavenly Father, thank You for Your sustaining mercy, grace, strength, and love that carries us throughout our lives. Forgive us for not thirsting for You. Ignite our passion and desire to know You. In Jesus' name, amen.

**Thought for the Day:** Make a conscious effort to pursue God as you walk through your day.

## Day 3: Peace

by Shirley
Read Psalm 119:161-168

*Great peace have those who love your law;*
*nothing can make them stumble.*
Psalm 119:165

I love peaceful rivers and rainfall in the summer.

One hot, humid summer day, some friends and I were hiking in the woods. We had come well-prepared with water so we wouldn't get dehydrated. After about thirty minutes of hiking up a mountain—okay, it was probably just a hill—we sat down in the shade of a tree to rest and drink some water. Everyone was tired and out of breath, so we weren't talking. One of the guys decided to hike ahead to determine the best way for us to proceed. All of a sudden he started yelling, "Hey guys. Come on up here, it is beautiful."

We moaned and groaned a bit, but got up and started following the sound of his voice. As we reached a little bit of a plateau, we saw our friend's shoes and socks on the ground, and then saw him wading into a beautiful river. We quickly took off our shoes and socks and joined him.

The water was clear and very cold. After spending time wading, cooling down, and getting soaking wet, we sat down on the plateau to dry off, eat our lunch, and rest. The sound of the flowing river was very relaxing.

After months of dry season in Nigeria, the rainfall was such a welcome relief from the heat and dryness. The same holds true in the States after periods of drought. It isn't often that I go out and play in and celebrate the rain now as I did when I was a child in Nigeria.

You can almost hear the sighs of relief and refreshment as the dry and cracked earth soaks up the rain. The birds come out and splash in the puddles left by the rain. The trees seem to shake off all the dust and stand up a little straighter after a good rainfall.

As I was having supper one day with a friend and telling her about this summer devotional, she introduced me to a hymn, *Peace*, by Barney E.

Warren.

Let's look at the lyrics of this hymn.

Sweet peace is flowing, peace that
will abide;
Peace e'er increasing, Jesus will
provide;
Peace like a river in the time of
drouth,
Flowing on forever, from the sunny
south.

Refrain:
Peace, peace, wonderful peace!
Flowing so deep in my soul;
Peace, peace, sweet peace,
How it maketh the sad heart whole.

My friend explained that the foundational verse for this hymn is found in today's key passage from an eight-verse stanza of Psalm 119. It describes the spiritual warfare in which the Psalmist is engaged. Love for God's word and His hope in God's deliverance result in him experiencing peace in midst of the battle because he follows God's commands. He trusts that God is in control and will keep him from stumbling.

Juxtapose the result of the Israelites not paying attention to God's word. "Oh that you had paid attention to my commandments! Then your peace would have been like a river, and your righteousness like the waves of the sea" (Isaiah 48:18).

The stanza speaks of the showers God sends our way.

Sweet peace in Jesus, never can be
told;
Oh, it is glorious, better far than
gold;
Showers are falling all around me
here,
Peace that is amazing, desert hearts
to cheer.

God sends the showers from heaven that bear the fruit of righteousness in our lives, as we see in the prayer for deliverance in Isaiah 45:8. "Shower,

O heavens, from above, and let the clouds rain down righteousness; let the earth open, that salvation and righteousness may bear fruit; let the earth cause them both to sprout; I the LORD have created it."

> Come, weary sinner, thirsty you may be,
> Drink of the water Jesus offers thee;
> Oh, it will gladden like the summer rain,
> As the blooming Eden, you may then remain.

In John 4, Jesus encounters a Samaritan woman at a well. He tells her, "Everyone who drinks of this water will be thirsty again, but whoever drinks of the water that I will give him will never be thirsty again. The water that I will give him will become in him a spring of water welling up to eternal life" (John 4:13-14). This living water bubbles up within us as a result of the Holy Spirit's work in our hearts. This stanza says the living water will refresh and invigorate us like the rain after a long dry spell.

**Prayer:** Heavenly Father, help us love and obey Your word so that we will experience Your peace like a river. May we experience the refreshing living water You give. In Jesus' name, amen.

**Thought for the Day:** God's peace comes as a result of our unhindered relationship with Jesus Christ.

## Day 4: Revive Us Again

by Shirley
Read 2 Chronicles 7:11-18

*Will you not revive us again,*
*that your people may rejoice in you?*
Psalm 85:6

Many years ago my mom, my brother Tim, and I moved from separate homes/apartments into one large house. All three of us had a house full of furniture and stuff, so once we got moved into our new home we decided what pieces of furniture we needed and which pieces we would sell. We didn't need three formal dining room sets, nor multiples of various other items.

We sorted through and labeled all the items with prices. It was to be a two-day sale on Friday and Saturday. Those were sweltering days, and we wore ourselves out talking with people, showing them things, and helping them load their items.

The sale ended Saturday afternoon, and the

guys who were going to buy everything that hadn't sold yet, which wasn't much, came and we helped get their trucks loaded. I sat down on the front porch step and watched the last few items get loaded. Tim was going with the guys to help them unload everything, so I sat there and watched them leave.

I started to get up several times but I couldn't. I was hot, tired, and dirty from head to toe, and every muscle in my body was hurting. Mom brought me a glass of iced tea, and we sat together for a while talking about the day and the people who had come to the sale. Mom then got up and told me to get a shower and come help her get supper ready.

Although the sweet tea had helped perk me up a little, I still didn't have the energy to move. It wasn't long until Tim came back and found me sitting right where I was when he left. He asked, "Why didn't you go in and take a shower?"

"Because I can't move," I said.

He pulled me up and pulled me toward the bathroom and told me to get in the shower, that it would help me feel better. I started with cool water and then turned on the hot water to scrub all the sweat and dirt off. As I walked into the kitchen I was feeling much better, but still tired.

I helped Mom get supper ready and was moving slower than Mom thought I should. She started singing, “Revive us again. Fill each heart with thy love. May each soul be rekindled with fire from above.”

Tim came in from his shower and helped get all the food on the table. We sat down to eat and Mom prayed, “Lord, we’re exhausted. Thank You for the good sale and for bringing all the people here to buy our stuff. Thank You for the food. Revive us again.”

I didn’t think I was very hungry, but once I started eating, I realized I was starved—okay, maybe just real hungry. We talked through the events of the past several days of getting things ready for the sale and then handling the sale. We were pleased with the results of the sale—both the money we made and the things that we were able to clear out.

After supper we cleared the table, and we all seemed to have more energy to get the dishwasher loaded and the kitchen cleaned.

We had indeed been revived. Our tired bodies had been refreshed by a shower, food and drink, and relaxing fellowship and conversation. Mom, of course, made sure we noted that God revives us spiritually when we are complacent, tired, and heavy-laden with the guilt of our sin.

I often hear people say our churches need an old-fashioned revival. When you ask them to describe what they mean, they refer to an event that we used to schedule in our churches a couple of times a year. It seems that they think holding revival services will bring about revival.

Biblical revival is for those who already have new life in Christ. It is for Christ-followers who have disobeyed God and not honored Him. Spiritually they are tired, listless, and complacent.

Do you know William P. Mackay's hymn, *Revive Us Again*? In some hymnals it is called *We Praise Thee, O God.*

> We praise Thee, O God!
> For the Son of Thy love,
> For Jesus Who died,
> And is now gone above.

Hallelujah! Thine the glory.
Hallelujah! Amen.
Hallelujah! Thine the glory.
Revive us again.

We praise Thee, O God!
For Thy Spirit of light,
Who hath shown us our Savior,
And scattered our night.

All glory and praise
To the Lamb that was slain,
Who hath borne all our sins,
And hath cleansed every stain.

All glory and praise
To the God of all grace,
Who hast brought us, and sought us,
And guided our ways.

Revive us again;
Fill each heart with Thy love;
May each soul be rekindled
With fire from above.

This is a beautiful hymn of praise to God for all that God has done for us. In the same way our bodies needed reviving and refreshing when we were hot and tired, our spiritual lives need reviving. As we sing about all these things, we realize that when we fail to read, study, memorize, contemplate, and meditate on God's word, we lose our passion to serve Him, and we quickly give in to temptation and sin. That realization leads us to ask God to revive us again so that our spiritual lives are restored and our love for God is renewed.

**Prayer:** Heavenly Father, "revive us again; fill each heart with Thy love; may each soul be rekindled with fire from above." In Jesus' name, amen.

**Thought for the Day:** The Lord stands ready to forgive your sin and revive you so that your soul is restored, refreshed, and eager to serve Him.

## Day 5: Jesus Shall Reign

by Shirley
Read Psalm 72

*"The LORD will reign forever and ever."*
Exodus 15:18

I was at the ICU waiting room sitting with a friend whose husband had a massive stroke. We weren't talking much, just sitting and waiting. I learned from an elderly gentleman sitting at the far end of the waiting room that his great-grandson had been seriously injured in a motorcycle accident. I noted various family members coming in and out. All of them were anxious and obviously distraught. The great-granddad, who they called Great Bert, sat comfortably in his chair and listened as people cried and talked about his great-grandson, (we'll call him J), being paralyzed, and they wondered how they could take care of an invalid and so many other things. One lady asked, "How will we get through this?"

Great Bert bowed his head and in a loud voice prayed, “Father, we know that you are here with us and we are comforted because Jesus reigns.”

That was a sweet prayer, but I don’t think some of the family were Christ-followers because they started right up saying, “He is going to be completely paralyzed. How can I be comforted?”

Great Bert bowed his head and prayed, “Gracious Father, help us trust You as You reign over this situation.”

On and on this type of exchange went as various family members came and went. The Isaac Watts hymn, *Jesus Shall Reign*, kept rolling over in my mind as I was composing an email.

I sent the email and realized the waiting room was completely silent, even though there were about twenty people in there. Great Bert was looking straight at me as he walked toward me and said, “That’s one of my favorites, I guess you can tell.” I was confused and didn’t understand what he meant, so I asked, “What is one of your favorites?”

“The hymn you were humming. I’ve been singing it over and over in my mind to remind me that God is in control. Would you sing it with me?”

I realized I wasn't just thinking the words of the hymn in my mind; I had been humming the tune loudly enough that the entire waiting room had heard me.

I asked Great Bert if I needed to pull up the words on my phone and he said, "Only if you need them," which I didn't. He sat beside me, took hold of my hand, and we sang,

Jesus shall reign where'er the sun
does its successive journeys run,
his kingdom stretch from shore to
shore,
till moons shall wax and wane no
more.

My friend looked up the words on her phone and started singing with us, as did several others in the waiting room.

To him shall endless prayer be
made,
and praises throng to crown his
head.

His name like sweet perfume shall
    rise
with every morning sacrifice.

People and realms of every tongue
dwell on his love with sweetest
    song,
and infant voices shall proclaim
their early blessings on his name.

Tears ran down Great Bert's face as he boldly sang,

Blessings abound where'er he
    reigns:
the prisoners leap to lose their
    chains,
the weary find eternal rest,
and all who suffer want are blest.

Great Bert regained his composure, stood and sang loudly,

Let every creature rise and bring

> the highest honors to our King,
> angels descend with songs again,
> and earth repeat the loud amen.

Great Bert grabbed my hand and my friend's hand and prayed loudly, thanking God that He was with us and our loved ones. He prayed the Lord would guide the medical teams as they treated our loved ones. He prayed that we would continually remember that Jesus reigns in every situation, everywhere, all the time. He prayed that the Lord would be gracious to J and allow him another opportunity to come to Christ.

The days that followed brought total healing to my friend's husband as he took his last breath here on earth and went to heaven to be with His Savior.

I kept in touch with Great Bert so I could check on how things were going. J stunned all the specialists as he began to move his legs and arms and speak without slurring his words. But Great Bert was not surprised at all, because he had asked God to give J one more opportunity to come to know Him.

I got a call from Great Bert asking if I could

come and be in J's room praying while he shared the gospel with him. It was a precious moment as Great Bert told J that he prayed God would be merciful and give him one more chance to come to Christ. He then shared the gospel in the most loving and gentle way. J said, "Great Bert, that's not my thing, you know that."

Great Bert took J's hand and prayed aloud. "Father, if I could confess and repent for this dear one I would. Thank You for your mercy to allow him to hear the gospel one last time. We gave him to you when we first learned he was just a few cells in his mommy's belly. I lay him in your hands now, trusting You to carry us through whatever is ahead."

He leaned over and kissed his J on the forehead and said, "Goodbye dear one, I'm sad that I may never see you again here on earth or for eternity."

I was sobbing as Great Bert and I walked out of that room. When I saw Great Bert's number on my phone the next morning my heart stopped, and I braced to hear the news that J had died. When I said, "Hello." I was greeted with a shout of "Hallelujah. The Lord saved him!"

I learned that Great Bert's pastor visited J not long after we left his room. The pastor prayed with him and shared the gospel. The Holy Spirit got hold of him and he repented of his sin and asked Jesus to save him.

The pastor got Great Bert on the phone so he could hear from J what happened. J said, "Jesus saved me," and all the alarms in the room started going off. The pastor grabbed his phone and stepped into the hallway and told Great Bert what was going on. Within minutes, J was with his Savior.

Great Bert said, "You see, Jesus reigns over everything."

Until this series of events, I usually heard this hymn sung in connection with mission conferences. It now has a different meaning for me as God enabled Great Bert to teach me and the watching world that Jesus reigns in every situation, everywhere, all the time.

**Prayer:** Heavenly Father, thank You for giving hymn writers the ability to put Your word to music so that it helps us renew our minds and strength and our faith as we sing to You. In Jesus' name, amen.

**Thought for the Day:** Regardless of what you are facing at this moment, you can be certain that Jesus is reigning over every situation, everywhere, all the time.

Chapter 5

# Happy Birthday, America!

## Day 1: Free Indeed

by Shirley
Read John 8:31-38

*And you will know the truth, and the truth will set you free . . . So if the Son sets you free, you will be free indeed.*
John 8:32, 36

When you think of Independence Day, July 4th, what comes to mind? Maybe you think of not having to go to work, a picnic or barbecue with family and friends, a fireworks display, or US flags dotting yards and streets.

Independence and freedom come to my mind. The Constitution of the United States of America ensures that every person has certain rights that no government, regardless of its power, can take away. If you haven't read the Preamble to the Constitution in a while, look it up online and read it.

I get frustrated when I see people not respecting the flag of the United States, for it is the emblem of our nation and the freedoms we enjoy. It reminds us of the many men and women who died to secure and maintain our freedom, and I am grateful for those sacrifices. Yet, the very thing our flag represents—independence and freedom—is the reason people do not have to respect our flag.

Let's see what Merriam-Webster says about these words. Freedom is "the power or right to act, speak, or think as one wants without hindrance or restraint." Independence is being "free from outside control; not depending on another's authority."

Our independence and freedom can bring out the best in all of us, and sadly, it can also bring out the worst in all of us.

America was built by independent thinkers who fought for the right to "act, speak, or think" as they wanted to "without hindrance or restraint." Many of those who fought for us sacrificed much—many gave their lives—to ensure our independence and freedom.

As American citizens we are free to worship—at least for now—in any way we choose, and as Christ-followers we know that the only real freedom we have is through a relationship with Jesus Christ.

Jesus tells us, "Everyone who practices sin is a

slave to sin" (John 8:34). Galatians 5:1 says, "For freedom Christ has set us free; stand firm therefore, and do not submit again to a yoke of slavery." Because Christ redeemed us, "The blood of Jesus his Son cleanses us from all sin" (1 John 1:7b).

What does our freedom in Christ mean? It is spiritual freedom from the bondage of our sin. It means we are free from the penalty of the law that we cannot keep because Jesus Christ paid that penalty on the cross. When we come to saving faith in Christ, we are free from the vain struggles of trying to please God in our flesh.

2 Corinthians 3:16-18 says it this way:

> "But when one turns to the Lord, the veil is removed. Now the Lord is the Spirit, and where the Spirit of the Lord is, there is freedom. And we all, with unveiled face, beholding the glory of the Lord, are being transformed into the same image from one degree of glory to another. For this comes from the Lord who is the Spirit."

As Christ-followers, we are free to become all God wants us to be by being faithful followers as we walk with Him. So, our freedom in Christ does have us under the authority of God and His word. We can rejoice in the freedom, protection, and blessings that come from obeying God. We are grateful for God's grace that enables us to obey Him.

Christ-followers are created in the image of God in order to reflect Him in everything we do and say. As we read, study, memorize, contemplate, and memorize Scripture, we come to know Him better and understand who He is and what He requires of us. As we live out God's commands, those around us get a glimpse of who He is, and the blessings of being free in Him.

**Prayer:** Heavenly Father, thank You for the freedoms we enjoy as Americans. Give us a passion to better represent You and the freedom we have in Christ to our sinful nation. Have mercy on us, Lord, and send a revival in our hearts that might spread through our nation and the world. In Jesus' name, amen.

**Thought for the Day:** On Independence Day, let's celebrate the independence and freedoms that make America unique from any other country in the world.

# Day 2: Sweet Freedom

by Harriet
Read John 8:31-36, Galatians 5:1

*And you shall know the truth, and the truth will set you free.*
John 8:32

Happy birthday, America! On July 4, 1776, our forefathers declared their freedom from English rule by signing the Declaration of Independence. This was no easy thing to do. War ensued. Many of the men who put their signatures on that paper suffered greatly for their brave act.

A quick Internet search found the following: five signers were captured and tortured before being killed, the homes of twelve were ransacked and then burned, two had sons captured during the Revolutionary War, and two more had sons that were killed during the war. One had a wife jailed by the British, and she died within a few months. Nine fought during the war and later died as a direct result of the war, either from wounds they received or other hardships caused by the war.

Our nation and the freedoms we enjoy came at a price. They are offered freely to us today, but many through the years have paid dearly so that we can enjoy them.

Jesus spoke of freedom several times in the Scripture. Perhaps the most often quoted was when he said the words recorded in our key verse, ". . . you will know the truth, and the truth will set you free" (John 8:32). At the time Jesus spoke these words, His disciples lived under Roman rule. Rome gave the Jewish people a large amount of autonomy, but they were all still keenly aware of the fact that they were not a completely free people. They also lived in a society where slavery existed, so even though none of the disciples were slaves, they understood the concept of being a slave and having to do whatever an owner demanded.

However, when Jesus spoke these words, He was not referring to national freedom. Rather, His remarks were aimed at spiritual freedom that comes from having our sins washed away by His blood and following Him. We know His remarks referred to spiritual freedom from sins based on other things

He said, both at this same time and at other times. Earlier, in verse 24 of this eighth chapter of John, Jesus said, "I told you that you would die in your sins, for unless you believe that I am he you will die in your sins." When Jesus said, "I am he," He meant that He was the Messiah whom God had sent to save people from eternal separation from God. Jesus tied this lack of knowing Him to freedom and slavery when He said in verses 34-35 that everyone who sins is a slave, and a slave has no part in the family; but, a son belongs to the family forever. Then He made another oft-quoted statement about freedom in verse 36 when He said, "he who the son sets free is free indeed."

Like our national freedom, our spiritual freedom was not free. It is offered freely to us, but it cost Jesus everything.

During these hot summer days when we shoot off fireworks to celebrate our nation and the freedoms we possess because of the great sacrifices of others, let's pause, at least for a few minutes, and thank God for our spiritual freedom and the sacrifice Jesus made to secure it.

"But thanks be to God that, though you used to

be slaves to sin, you have come to obey from your heart . . . You have been set free from sin . . ." Romans 6:17-18 (NIV).

**Prayer:** Heavenly Father, we thank You for the freedoms we enjoy both personally and spiritually. They are all gifts from You. Even those who do not live in nations where they can be free can have spiritual freedom in You. Thank You for setting us free from sin, and thank You for America. In Jesus' name, amen.

**Thought for the Day:** He who the Son sets free is free indeed.

## Day 3: Good Soldiers

by Shirley
Read Ephesians 6:10-20

*For we do not wrestle against flesh and blood,*
*but against the rulers, against the authorities, against the*
*cosmic powers over this present darkness,*
*against the spiritual forces of evil in the heavenly places.*
Ephesians 6:12

Thinking about the war that won America's independence from Great Britain has me thinking about soldiers. When we were growing up in Nigeria, my brothers and I were always playing soldiers. Sometimes we would play with other missionary kids and divide up into two or three different groups representing Nigerian tribes that would be fighting each other. Our guns were sticks or brooms—if we could sneak one out of the house. We would use rotten guavas as hand grenades. The goal was for one of the kings to rule over the others. The teams were usually Ogbomosho, Keffi, Lagos, and sometimes Zaria. We also had extensive cities built using Matchbox cars and various other things. These would be spread throughout several different rooms. The object was for one group of soldiers to capture one of the kings.

Let's look at some of the things I learned about soldiering from these childhood games.

- Soldiers have someone in charge of them who they obey and to whom they are loyal followers. Interestingly enough, in our games, girls were just as likely to be the generals and kings as the boys were.
- Soldiers are to obey orders quickly and without grumbling. Our grumbling had consequences, like being traded as a prisoner to an opposing side.
- Soldiers are to give their best at all times. Slackers in our war games were court-martialed and had to do the chores another soldier was assigned to do at home.
- Soldiers must be well-equipped for carrying out their jobs. That would include weapons, protective armor, intelligence about the other side, etc. So,

the person climbing trees to report the position of the other soldiers was usually a nimble climber.

- Soldiers must pay attention and be focused on the battle, and not be distracted. One time, a missionary kid rode his bicycle right into the middle of our battlefield. My brother Tim started talking with him and was bombarded by grenades (rotten guavas).

As I think about those soldier games, I realize that the same lessons I learned about soldiering apply to our lives as soldiers of Jesus Christ. The Bible speaks of soldiers and their armor. In today's passage, we read: "Therefore take up the whole armor of God that you may be able to withstand in the evil day, and having done all, to stand firm" (Ephesians 6:13).

Paul gives Timothy some instruction on how to be a good soldier of Jesus Christ in 2 Timothy 2:3-4: "Share in suffering as a good soldier of Christ Jesus. No soldier gets entangled in civilian pursuits, since his aim is to please the one who enlisted him."

- Soldiers of Christ have been enlisted by Jesus Christ, our commander who we obey and to whom we are loyal.
- Soldiers of Christ are to exercise their spiritual muscles so they are battle-ready and able to withstand the hardships that will come their way. They won't turn and run at the first sign of threats from the enemy.
- Soldiers of Christ are to please the Lord by obeying His commands and sharing the gospel with all those with whom we come in contact.
- Soldiers of Christ are not to be distracted by the things going on around them in their lives or the lives of others. Nor are they to be distracted by the temptations that come from the evil one or from their own lusts.
- Soldiers of Christ want to please Jesus Christ by faithfully serving and obeying His commands.

In his great hymn, *Soldiers of Christ Arise*, Charles Wesley describes the duty of a soldier of

Christ. Let's look at the third stanza:

Leave no unguarded place,
No weakness of the soul,
Take every virtue, every grace,
And fortify the whole.
From strength to strength go on,
Wrestle and fight and pray,
Tread all the pow'rs of darkness down
And win the well-fought day.

Here, we see that a soldier of Christ fortifies himself with every virtue and every grace as he wrestles, fights, and prays to stamp down all the powers of darkness.

**Prayer:** Heavenly Father, help us to be good soldiers for You. In Jesus' name, amen.

**Thought for the Day:** "Stand then in His great might, with all His strength endued, and take, to arm you for the fight, the panoply of God."[3]

---

[3] Charles Wesley. *Trinity Psalter Hymnal*, 1749, p. 540.

## Day 4: Love Your Enemies

by Harriet
Read Matthew 25:34-40

*But I say to you, love your enemies*
*and pray for those who persecute you.*
Matthew 5:44

My husband has a close friend from Germany. In high school, they both participated in student foreign exchange programs and ended up living at each other's homes for several months. My husband lived with his German friend for only three months in Munich, but his friend lived with him for a full year. Naturally, the two became life-long friends.

Shortly after my husband and I were married, we decided to visit his German "family." Sitting around visiting one night, I heard the friend's father, whom everyone called Vati—the German word for father—tell this story.

Vati had served in the German army in World

War II. He was only nineteen years old when he was forced into the German army, and he did not know or understand everything we now know about his country's wicked leader. He was drafted, so he served.

Toward the end of the war, in the middle of winter, Vati was captured by the Americans. He said he and a friend came upon an open, snow-covered field. The friend set out across it and managed to successfully cross, so Vati tried as well. Soon, he found himself apprehended by several armed American soldiers.

The soldiers ordered him to drop to his knees and put his hands up. Then they surrounded him and pointed their guns directly at his head. He knelt in the snow, expecting to be shot . . . but he was not.

Instead the soldiers told him to come with them to a nearby prisoner of war camp the Americans had made in the woods near the open field.

"Oh," he thought, "they will torture me before they kill me."

"Sit down," the Americans ordered when they arrived at camp, as they pointed to a log on the ground near a campfire. Vati obeyed, fearing what would happen next. He could feel the warmth of the fire, the first warmth of any kind he had experienced in weeks. He was tired, hungry and cold. He had not eaten in days, his coat was threadbare, and his boots so worn, his sockless toes were exposed. Even though he fully believed he was about to be tortured, for that brief moment, he warmed himself by the roaring fire.

As he waited, a US soldier brought him a bowl of hot soup and a spoon. Shortly thereafter, they gave him new boots and a new coat.

My eyes teared up as I heard this man say, "They did not torture me. They gave me shelter, warm clothes, and food."

What a testament to my nation. I swelled with national pride as I heard how my fighting men treated their captured enemies. Vati ended his story by saying, "If I had known this was what it was like to be captured by the Americans, I would have surrendered much earlier."

May God continue to bless America, and may we as a nation and as individuals remember to treat even our enemies with love.

**Prayer**: Heavenly Father, today's Scripture instructs us to be kind to others, even those who are not loving to us and even those who persecute us. Thank You for this story of a kindness shown that impacted a man for the rest of his life. May we be people who show kindness to others that You have brought into our lives. In Jesus name, amen.

**Thought for the Day**: Love your enemies. Pray for those who persecute you.

## Day 5: Remember and Teach

by Shirley
Read Deuteronomy 6:1-9

*He established a testimony . . .*
*he commanded our fathers to teach to their children,*
*that the next generation might know them*
*so . . . that they should set their hope in God*
*and not forget the works of God.*
Psalm 78:5-7

As a missionary kid, I consider Nigeria, West Africa, and the United States of America my "homes," and I love both of them. They hold special places in my heart. I am grateful for the experiences, some very positive and some negative, that I had growing up in Nigeria. And, I am grateful that I live in America, even with all of her faults and problems.

My dad loved America, the country for which he fought during World War II as a Navy Corpsman attached to the Third Marine Division on Guam and Iwo Jima. He loved the flag of the United States and taught us to love and respect it as a symbol of

America and a symbol of freedom. Throughout the years, many men and women have fought for us, maintaining our freedoms.

Countless times, I heard my dad speak of how the US flag gave hope and spurred on those Marines on Iwo Jima as it was raised on top of the volcano, Mount Surabachi. After the first smaller flag was raised, they raised a second, larger flag so it could be clearly seen on the island down below and by those on the ships in nearby waters. That moment was captured by Joe Rosenthal in the now-famous picture of the Marines raising the second flag.

Dad taught me how important it is to remember the sacrifices made not only by those who fought in World War II, but by all those service men and women who have fought for our nation. My friend, Dr. Howard Eyrich, encourages us to do our children and our nation a favor by taking time to explain the reason behind our patriotic celebrations. It is important for our children to know why it is important for us to remember how Americans gained and have maintained our freedoms—through the sacrifices of many brave men and women who fought for us.

My dad and Dr. Eyrich understood the importance of remembering the sacrifices made to secure our freedom and of teaching the next generations what happened and why it happened, as well as expressing thankfulness for their sacrifices. Hopefully, as we remember the things that happened in the past, we will come to love our country. Dr. Eyrich said it well, “We would do well to take a lesson from Moses—remember and teach.”

In today’s passage, Moses tells the Israelites to teach their children, who would teach their children, who would teach their children, and so on, making sure they passed their faith along for generations to come. That is precisely what we are to do today.

Christ-followers are to know and obey the commandments of God. As Christ-following parents live out the word of God, by their example they are teaching their children how to “love the LORD your God with all your heart and with all your soul and with all your might” (Deuteronomy 6:5).

Parents are also to be diligent to teach the word

of God to their children. This is in the "as you go about" sense. This means at the breakfast or dinner table, traveling in the car, when you are putting your children to bed, when you are working in the yard, wherever you are with your children.

Our passage from Psalms tells us to pass along our knowledge and understanding of God to the next generation so that they will come to know the word of God and "set their hope in God and not forget the works of God."

Remembering the works of God and knowing the word of God help the next generation come to a saving knowledge of Him, to trust Him, and to obey Him. It would also help them not to become stubborn and rebellious like their fathers.

Many people today are trying to rewrite American history so it justifies their agenda for the present and future. Many are trying to remove anything that points to God and to limit our freedom that we have as Americans to worship freely. Regardless of these things, God's word will remain strong in the hearts of His people. Our nation was indeed founded by men and women, flawed and sinful as they were, who placed their trust and hope in God.

**Prayer:** Heavenly Father, as we reflect upon the current state of our nation and world, we thank You for the abundant life we have in Your Son, Jesus, and for the gracious blessings we enjoy as Americans. May we be beacons of the Light and Hope of God—our only hope for us individually, for our nation, and the world—our risen Savior, Jesus Christ. In Jesus' name, amen.

**Thought for the Day:** Are you teaching the next generation to remember the sacrifice of Jesus, who purchased our redemption, and the sacrifices of countless men and women through the years who fought for the freedoms we Americans enjoy?

Chapter 6

# Vacation Fun

## Day 1: Fun Times

by Harriet
Read Proverbs 8:30-31, Psalm 149:4

*Delight yourself in the LORD,*
*and he will give you the desires of your heart.*
Psalm 37:4

From what I've been told, my father-in-law, David Michael, was a fun person to be around. He delighted in life and helped those around him to find the fun side of life, too.

I never knew my father-in-law. He was killed in a private plane crash when my husband was only sixteen, but the memories of him live on. I've seen pictures of him. He had a huge smile. My mother-in-law used to say his smile literally stretched from one ear to the other. One of my sons inherited this trait, and a person can't help but feel better just seeing someone with a smile that wide on his face. David laughed hard and often, too.

He and my mother-in-law met and fell in love

at Brown University, where he was a stand-out athlete, who today has been inducted into Brown's Athletic Hall of Fame for both soccer and wrestling. He is the person who led my mother-in-law to Christ, something that impacts me directly, since they reared their children in the fear and admonition of the Lord. His coming to follow Jesus is something that will bless my family for generations to come.

He had an adventurous spirit. An entrepreneur, he started a business that made oil and greases for coal-mining machinery, and he became quite successful. When he died, he left his wife a small business that supported her for years until she sold it and then lived off the income from the money she made on the sale.

Because his business owned a small plane, which he knew how to fly, he took his family on fishing trips, hunting trips, and a lot of vacation trips. My husband tells of flying near a flock of flamingos once, in the Bahamas, and seeing a mass of pink outside his window. They also owned a houseboat on a lake in West Virginia and spent many fun family days there.

Because he owned his own business, he could take off work any time he wanted to, as long as the operations manager that he had hired stayed behind to cover things in his absence. Even back in the days before computers and cell phones, he could stay in touch by telephone and knew he could come back to work immediately if a problem developed. And when he worked, he worked hard.

He worked hard, and he played hard.

Once, the newspaper in the small town in Illinois where he lived interviewed him. I've seen a clipping of that interview. They mostly asked him about his business, as it employed some of the residents and helped the local economy, but they also asked him about how he liked to spend his vacations. My father-in-law answered, "My whole life's a vacation." He meant that, too. That statement was a good portrayal of his outlook on life. He found things daily to delight in. He delighted in life.

In today's Scripture readings, we read a lot about delighting. Our key verse, Psalm 37:4, talks about us delighting in God, and one of our reading passages, Psalm 149:4, says that God takes pleasure in His people. He delights in us.

The word "fun" can sometimes take on a negative connotation, sadly, implying activities that are not wholesome or pure. But the truth is, there is much to delight us in this amazing world that God has made; good, wholesome, pure, and beautiful things that God has made. There is fun to be had all around us, every day.

**Prayer:** Gracious Father, You created us and placed us in a marvelous world that You made to give us sustenance, abundance, and joy. Thank You. May we learn to delight in You and the works of Your hands, even as You delight in us. In Jesus' name, amen.

**Thought for the Day:** All of life's a vacation. Have fun.

## Day 2: We Took God on Vacation

by Shirley
Read 1 Corinthians 11:23-26

*I will remember the deeds of the LORD;*
*Yes, I will remember your wonders of old.*
Psalm 77:11

Sitting in a restaurant eating lunch one Sunday afternoon, I overheard an exchange between family members—a grandmother, father, mother, and two children who were about eight and eleven years old. The grandmother was asking the other family members to tell her about the vacation from which they had just returned.

Grandmother said, “Tell me about your vacation.” Since both children tried to talk at the same time and talk louder than the other, the grandmother suggested that they go in turn from father, to mother, to oldest child (boy), to youngest child (girl). Further, she gave suggested topics for each one to tell about. The father was to tell his overall impressions of the vacation, the mom was to tell about what she enjoyed the most about the vacation, the boy was to tell the most exciting thing they did, and the girl was to tell what she remembered the most about their vacation.

Their meal arrived, and they all bowed their heads in prayer as the father thanked the Lord for his family, for looking after his mom while they were gone, for the time they had had together as a family, and for the food.

The father talked about how expensive everything was, from clothing and all the other things that had to be purchased for the vacation, to gasoline for the trip, to meals, lodging, and activities. The mother talked about how exhausting it was to get everything bought, packed, and ready for the family to leave on vacation, but also about how the change in routine gave her extra time to complete reading two books she took with her. She added that any relaxing she had done disappeared as she spent the entire Saturday evening getting all the laundry done and put away and making sure everyone's clothes were put out and ready for church the next morning.

As the boy began talking, I noticed the girl had turned her kids' coloring sheet over and was writing things with her purple crayon. She was not listening to her brother, but instead seemed to be concentrating hard, trying to remember things to write down.

The boy talked about the new video game he had gotten just before vacation and how he had mastered a bunch of different levels. He talked about the amazing things this game had that he had never seen in a video game, and how he really liked how the game made him feel when he mastered a level. Apparently, the screen lit up with bright colors while upbeat music played in the background, and the game congratulated him with phrases like, “What an awesome player.” “You did it.” “Don’t stop now.”

The father got the girl’s attention and said, “It’s your time now, sweetheart.” The little girl folded the bottom of the sheet so that the last thing she wrote was covered up in the fold. She handed her coloring sheet to her dad, who was sitting beside her, and pointed to the things she had written on the back as her non-verbal expressions nudged him to read what she wrote. Her father reached over and put his daughter's hand in his and said, "Would you like to read it with me?" The daughter pointed to the first thing on her list, and her dad read, "We took God on vacation with us." The rest of the family had confused looks on their faces as the father read it again. Her grandmother said, "Oh? Tell me about that."

The girl leaned toward her father to get a better look at her list and then began speaking. It was then that I realized she talked with a stutter. It took her quite a while to read, "We forgot to take our puzzles." Then she read, "M (her brother) let me talk as much as I wanted."

At this point she took a deep breath and looked at her dad and said, "Will you tell my memory?" Dad proceeded to read about eight other things that were on her list. "I love ice cream, did not eat ice cream." The list continued with seemingly random thoughts about what happened.

Dad looked at his daughter and asked if he should unfold the sheet and read what was there. She nodded yes. Dad read, "We talked to God. We listened to God talk. We talked about God. We sang to God. We said thank You to God. We clapped for God doing a good job making the ocean and the sun."

Grandmother, father, and mother were teary-eyed, and so was I. The boy said, "You make it sound like God was everywhere we went." The little girl's eyes lit up and she smiled broadly as she said, with barely a trace of stutter, "We took God on vacation and that made it great."

Let that sink in for a few moments. Even though the parents talked at lunch about the cost and hard work to prepare for and settle in after their vacation, they apparently ensured they communicated with God through prayer and Bible reading, talked about God and His creation, and made God an integral part of their family's vacation.

Sadly, many of us make meticulous plans for our vacations, giving little thought to "taking God with us" so that during our vacations our family is fed spiritually and able to rest in and enjoy God.

The Old Testament is filled with passages that tell us to remember what God did for His people. Remembering these things helps assure Christ-followers that they can walk into any situation with the confidence that God is with them.

Read the passage about Jesus telling His disciples to partake of the Lord's Supper and remember His death, burial, and resurrection. Today, as we remember all that He has done, is doing, and will do for us, it gives us boldness, confidence, and strength to face whatever comes our way throughout the day.

**Prayer:** Heavenly Father, thank You for the Bible, through which we are reminded who You are and what You have done. Thank You that as we revisit memories of our lives, we can see Your ever-present mercy, grace, and love. Lord, by Your Spirit, indelibly burn these memories into our hearts so that we never forget. In Jesus' name, amen.

**Thought for the Day:** How are you creating memories each day about which your family will say, "We took God on vacation, and that made it great."

## Day 3: A Hike Through Matthew

by Harriet
Read Matthew 28:16-20

*I lift my eyes to the hills. . . .*
Psalm 121:1a

Do you prefer vacations at the beach or in the mountains? If you said mountains, what do you like to do there? Do you ever go on hikes? For today's devotion, we are going to take a hike through the mountains of the book of Matthew. Not a real hike, obviously, but a word-trip to the mountains mentioned in Matthew, to learn a little about each.

**The Mountain of Temptation**

In Matthew 4:8, Satan took Jesus to the top of a very high mountain and showed Him all the kingdoms of the world. There the devil tempted Jesus, promising to give Him all the kingdoms if only Jesus would worship him. Because the Bible doesn't tell us the name of this mountain, we don't know exactly where it is. All we know is that it was a very high mountain.

Of course, Jesus refused to worship Satan. Although He was tempted, Jesus did not sin.

**The Mountain Where a Sermon Took Place**

A mountain is seen again in the next chapter of Matthew—chapter 5. This time it was a small mountain near the city of Capernaum and instead of being tempted, Jesus preached what is often referred to as "The Sermon on the Mount," the sermon of Jesus that contained the Beatitudes—a list of conditions under which a person is blessed. Again, the Bible doesn't tell us the name of this mountain; just that it was near the city of Capernaum.

**The Mountain of a Miracle**

Jesus is once again on a mountain in Matthew 15:29-39. On this mountain, He worked a miracle. He fed 5,000 people with only the lunch of one little boy; just five little loaves of bread and two small fish. It was lunch time and the people were hungry, so Jesus told them to sit down and they obeyed

Him. Then he kept breaking up the little bit of available food and sharing it. Miraculously, there was enough to feed all the people with twelve baskets left over. We do not know the name of this mountain either, but we know it was located near the Sea of Galilee.

**The Mountain of Transfiguration**

Matthew 17:1-9 tells about the "Mount of Transfiguration" as it is called, and the miracle that occurred there. In this story, Jesus took three of His disciples with Him up to a mountain and his appearance changed right before their eyes. His face shone like the sun, and His clothes became as white as snow. Moses and Elijah appeared with Jesus and began to talk to Him, too. The three disciples stood near Jesus and watched in amazement.

I can only imagine how the disciples felt when they saw Jesus changed like this. Did His brightness hurt their eyes? Maybe their jaws dropped open and their eyes widened.

**The Mountain of Olives**

In Matthew 24, Jesus is on a mountain, and this time the Bible tells us its name. It is identified as the Mount of Olives. Here, Jesus told the crowd listening to Him about His second coming; the time when He will return to the earth again.

**The Mountain of Ascension**

The final mountain can be found in the very last verses of Matthew after Jesus had been crucified and rose again. Here, He claimed to have all authority in heaven and earth, and He told His disciples to go into the world and tell others about Him in a passage that is often called "The Great Commission." Jesus' instructions were not just for His disciples; they were for us today, too. Then Jesus ascended to heaven from a mountain (Matthew 28:18-20).

Now, we have hiked up and down the many mountains mentioned in the gospel of Matthew that played a role in Jesus' life and ministry. This devotion was more of a Biblical geography lesson than a heart-touching, thought-provoking meditation, but it is always important to learn more about the context in which the things recorded in Scripture happened.

No need to hike a mountain trail this year on vacation now. We have just taken a mental hike through many.

**Prayer:** Heavenly Father, mountains were important to Jesus when He lived and ministered on this earth. This summer, whether we take a mountain vacation or not, open our eyes and teach us more about Your experiences on mountains. In Jesus' name, amen.

**Thought for the Day:** Spend more time today reading about the mountains mentioned in this devotional and the things that happened on them.

## Day 4: Are We There Yet?

by Shirley
Read Isaiah 40:27-31

*But they who wait for the LORD shall renew their strength;*
*they shall mount up with wings like eagles;*
*they shall run and not be weary;*
*they shall walk and not faint.*
Isaiah 40:31

I'm sure that every parent who read this devotional title giggled a little, thinking about his or her experiences traveling with children. When it came time for our vacation trips each summer in the States, we would all pack our bags and put everything we wanted to take out to the carport beside the car. Then, Mom and Dad would go through all the things we thought we needed to take and send us back into the house with whatever items they didn't think we would need. Then, Dad would figure out the best order in which to load each bag and the best place for it. It always amazed me that he could get it all in the trunk. Soon, we would be on our way.

It usually didn't take very long for me to ask Dad how long it would take to get to our destination. His usual response was, "It depends on how often we stop and how long we stay at each place we stop." I knew that meant that we would stop at every junk store—I mean antique store—we passed. We would also stop to get boiled peanuts or fresh fruit. And we would stop to see the "World's Greatest/Best" thing the billboards advertised. If we were going to the mountains, we would stop at the lookout spots and see the beauty of God's creation and when possible, we would take off our shoes and wade in cool—well, freezing cold—mountain streams. The further along into the trip we proceeded, the less excited Tim and I were to stop at yet another place to see anything.

We asked questions about the things we would see and do when we arrived at our destination. Admittedly, we weren't always excited about all the things that Mom and Dad planned for us to do, and we would start talking about how we wished we could do what we had done last year or the year before. We would go into detail about exactly what we did and how much fun it was. Now, we weren't really complaining—much.

Mom would remind us that once we got to our destination, we would enjoy the things they had planned, if we approached them with excitement and a ready-to-have-a-good-time attitude.

Inevitably I would ask, "Are we there yet? Can't you drive any faster?" Tim would just shake his head at me, and Dad would just raise his eyebrows a bit. Those questions were Mom's cue to suggest a game for us to play. We would see who saw the most different state license plates, the most blue (or whatever color) cars, the most of a certain make of cars, or the most different animals and birds. Sometimes we would play card games or sing songs. Before we knew it, we had arrived at our destination.

Mom was a master at keeping children occupied so they would not complain. In addition to teaching us different state, car, and tree names, she taught us to observe things going on around us and to look forward to what we would be doing in the future, whether we were excited about it or not.

Children, and adults, do not like having to wait for anything, do we? We often want to hurry things up and get to the next thing. Many times, we can't stand to just sit around and wait because we don't want to waste time, or we're afraid we'll miss out on something going on elsewhere. Nowadays, since we are rarely without our electronic devices, we can fill up the waiting time with social media, games, and reading.

In today's key passage we are told to "wait upon the Lord." According to Strong's Concordance, "wait" in Hebrew is *qavah*, which means "to wait, look for, hope, expect." So what exactly is our passage telling us to do? It is telling us to wait and watch expectantly for what God is going to do in our lives.

God uses our wait times to replenish, sanctify (make us more into His image), and prepare us for what He has in store. A handwritten note beside Isaiah 40:31 in my Bible says, "purposeful preparation."

I recently had an opportunity to share with a couple who parent young teens about my parents' purposeful preparation for our vacations back then, as well as for our future lives.

Let me explain. The stops at the antique/junktique shops were opportunities for Mom and Dad to tell us their memories of growing up using the items we would see, so we learned a lot of family history. We were exposed to many things that I have not seen since. We also gained appreciation for antiques as reminders of how much things had changed in the time since those things were used. We stopped to see the attractions the billboards called the "World's Greatest/Best" things, even when we knew that what the sign said about the thing could not be true. We didn't actually get to see many of the attractions because they cost too much, but we had fun looking and learning and laughing together. We learned not to be gullible and believe everything we read and heard.

We also learned that in our waiting we could learn and experience exciting and fun things. Most importantly, with every stop—particularly those that allowed us to soak up the beauty and majesty of God's creation—our parents taught us about the Creator God who loves, strengthens, sustains, and enables us to use our time wisely as we wait on Him. We learned to live in the moment and not be so anxious to get on to the next thing.

One time I asked the question, "Are we there yet?" and Mom answered, "Yes, we are." I looked around and could tell that we were not at our destination. My sigh of resignation was met with my mom's enthusiastic, "Yes, we are right where we are and ready to see what God has for us to enjoy."

In Psalm 27:14 we are told to "Wait for the Lord; be strong, and let your heart take courage; wait for the Lord." By God's mercy, grace, and strength, we can emerge from our waiting times refreshed, strengthened, and ready for whatever comes our way.

**Prayer:** Heavenly Father, thank You for the periods of waiting that enable us to learn to trust You more and learn more about You. Forgive us for getting so anxious for the next thing that we don't want to wait. During our waiting times, help us trust and rely upon You to replenish, sanctify, and prepare us for what lies ahead. In Jesus' name, amen.

**Thought for the Day:** "Wait at His door with prayer; wait at His foot with humility; wait at His table with service; wait at His window with expectancy."[4]

---

[4] Charles Spurgeon, *The Treasury of David: Volume II,* New York: I.K. Funk & Company, 1882, page 6.

## Day 5: Life's a Party!

by Harriet
Read Proverbs 15:1-4, 13,15

*A happy heart makes the face cheerful,*
*but heartache crushes the spirit.*
Proverbs 15:13 (NIV)

When my three oldest children were young, I attempted to teach them to put away their clean laundry. I tried to make it a required task, part of their weekly chores, which I insisted they do. I tried reminding them in a pleasant voice and in a stern voice, but the results were the same—they never wanted to do this task. They acted as if leaving their activities and coming to the laundry room to receive their laundry was a major imposition on them, not to mention then having to take the clean laundry upstairs to their rooms and put it away. It was not a fun experience for them or for me.

One day, for no particular reason, I headed toward the laundry room and said in a more chipper than usual voice, "Come on kids, let's have a laundry party."

Their response was golden. Three excited children ran to the laundry room, giggling as they eagerly held their arms out to receive their laundry. Playing along, as I handed each his or her stack of clean laundry, I said, "Party favors for you, and you and you." Then I watched them skip away upstairs to put their laundry in their drawers. I was left shaking my head, not believing what had just happened.

I tried it again the next week, and again and again, each following laundry day. It worked every time.

A few years ago, when my family had gathered to celebrate a family occasion of some kind, I overheard my now-grown son ask his sister, "Do you remember Mom's laundry parties when we were kids?"

She laughed in response. "Yeah," she said, "I always thought it was so much fun, like it really was a party of some kind. Now, of course, I realize she just said that to get us to put up laundry."

They both laughed, and so did I. But looking

back at it, I see a life-lesson buried in this experience. So much of how we perceive our situations in life has more to do with our reactions and attitudes about the things we encounter than with what actually happens to us.

These verses in Proverbs teach that point. Verse 15 says that a person with a cheerful heart will have a continual feast. A feast in those days was a big deal. It was sort of like a grand party. Today when we think of parties, we think of more than just enjoying good food. That's because food is readily available to us today with transportation that brings food into our grocery stores from all over the world, and with canning, freezing, and refrigeration techniques that can keep food fresh for long periods of time. But back then, food was a big deal, especially meat. Back then, a feast—a large table of deliciously prepared food—was a large celebration, enjoyed by all who found themselves invited.

Life is what we make of it. Our attitudes can make all the difference in how we perceive our situations. My kids proved this point. Laundry went from a chore to a party when their little hearts felt cheerful. Life can be a party, or a vacation, if we face our circumstances with cheerful hearts.

**Prayer:** Gracious Heavenly Father, You created us and blessed us in so many ways. Make us to recall Your goodness and teach our hearts to be cheerful. In Your name, amen.

**Thought for the Day:** It's all in the attitude!

Chapter 7

# The Dog Days of Summer

## Day 1: Dog Days of Summer

by Harriet
Read Jeremiah 17: 5-8

*Its rising is from the end of the heavens,*
*and its circuit to the end of them,*
*and there is nothing hidden from its heat.*
Psalm 19:6

Have you ever heard the term, "the dog days of summer?" If you're like me, you know it refers to the hottest parts of the summer, but why are they called "dog days?" How did we get this term?

The expression "dog days," meaning the hottest, sultry summer days, has a long history. It can be found being used as far back as the days of the Greek empire. They were not talking about dogs, the animal, but rather referred to a dog constellation in the night sky. It had many names, the most common being Sirius. This constellation that the Greeks thought formed the shape of a dog can be seen near the constellation Orion, so it is often referred to as Orion's dog.

Sirius's rise to prominence in the night sky always ushered in the hottest part of the summer. Thus the “dog days of summer” are those days when Sirius is prominent in the sky, and the days we are facing are hot, hot, hot.

The term continued to be used to indicate these hot summer days for centuries. For instance, in 1564 an English medical journal cautioned that certain medical practices they used at the time, such as bloodletting and inducing vomiting, which were deemed helpful back then to purge the body of illnesses, not be done during the dog days of summer because the heat made the body too weak to endure these practices.

My background is in nursing. I have a Bachelor of Science in Nursing, and though I roll my eyes at these ancient practices, I must at least give these ancient medical personnel a nod that they considered these practices contraindicated in the hot summer. These practices can easily cause dehydration which, of course, can be worse in the summer.

Now we know where the term comes from, but I must let my readers know that I am using the term quite loosely in this chapter and using it as a springboard to write devotions in which dogs play a significant role. Today's devotion, though, will deal with the summer heat as a symbol of a dry, wasted spiritual life and how to change things and withstand difficult circumstances that try to push us into spiritual droughts.

Our reading passage for today draws a clear distinction between those who place their trust in man and those who place their trust in God. It says that a person who places his trust in humans will be like a shrub that grows in parched places in an uninhabited, salty land. This is in stark contrast with a person who places his or her trust in God. According to verse 8, that person is like a tree planted near water. It does not worry about the heat because its leaves stay green even in the hottest heat, even in the dog days of summer.

This is, of course, symbolic of believers whose spiritual roots stay near the source of nourishment—God's word. Even when these Christ-followers face difficulties in their lives, they have a strength not of their own, a supernatural peace that passes understanding.

**Prayer:** Heavenly Father, You are the source of our nourishment. You make us able to withstand difficulties and to face every day, no matter what may come our way. Thank You for planting us near You and causing us to flourish even in tough times. In Jesus' name, amen.

**Thought for the Day:** Because of God, we can face the dog days of summer in our lives.

## Day 2: A Dog Named Kitty

by Harriet
Read Psalm 36:5-7

*The righteous care for the needs of their animals. . . .*
Proverbs 12:10a (NIV)

When I met my husband, John, he had a little dog he had named Kitty. Strange name for a dog. I asked him why he had named her that, and he said he meant it like the name one might call a girl or a woman. True, I have known women named Kitty in my life, but I still thought it a strange choice for a dog's name.

But Kitty was a sweet little dog and my husband loved her very much. She was a tiny black female toy poodle that he carried around with him everywhere. He had even taken her with him to college. Though he was just out of college when we met, he told me the story.

John's father had passed away unexpectedly in a plane crash when he was just sixteen years old, and Kitty, along with her two siblings, was born the year following his dad's death. The family owned Kitty's parents, but this particular litter ended up unusually small—more like teacup poodles than toy. Kitty turned out to weigh only three pounds, and he said the other two in the litter were even smaller. John asked for and was given Kitty as his own. When it came time to go to college just a year later, he petitioned and was granted special permission to bring her to college and keep her in his dorm room. I do not know why the school allowed it, but I'm sure the loss of his dad and her small size both played roles in the decision.

John kept that dog in his room for all of his years of college. She even walked beside him when he graduated—I've seen the pictures.

When I first met him, I did not know he had a dog. We met at church one Sunday morning after he moved near my hometown of Bluefield, West Virginia, to work following his graduation. He did not bring his dog to church, so that Sunday morning I had no idea he had a dog. But, I found him to be an interesting guy anyway. He asked me to lunch that day, and we started dating almost immediately.

He teased later telling me that he knew I was special because I was the first girl in a long time who had been attracted to him instead of his dog.

Ours was a whirlwind romance, and within just a few months we became engaged. That happened to be around Christmas time. We took a trip to my uncle and aunt's home for a large family gathering. Since the trip was long and involved an overnight stay, John brought Kitty with him. At the gathering, John met my cousins and their children. The children enjoyed playing with Kitty and with John.

Toward the end of our time there, my grandfather called me over to him to tell me something. Granddaddy, as I called him, was a hard-working farmer. He had spent his whole life working in a textile mill and farming his land. He did not have a formal education past the third grade, but he had wisdom that came from years of experience. I will always remember what he told me that day. He said, "I've been watching your John, and he's a good man. Any man that likes dogs and kids is a good man."

Whether he realized it or not, my grandfather spoke a biblical truth that day. Our key verse tells us that one indication of a righteous person is that he or she cares for the needs of his or her animals, whether they be farm animals or household pets. And Proverbs 27:23 tells us to be diligent to know how our flocks are doing. In other words, be diligent to know how those animals and people who may be under our charge are doing.

**Prayer:** Father, thank You for making animals. They bring us such joy and are helpful to us in so many ways. Yet, those we take into our home depend on us. Help us to be diligent to care for them as we should, much like the way You constantly provide for and take care of us. In Jesus' name, amen.

**Thought for the Day:** Do you know the state of your flock?

## Day 3: Laughter is the Best Medicine

by Harriet
Read Proverbs 15:13-15

*A joyful heart is good medicine,*
*but a crushed spirit dries up the bones.*
Proverbs 17:22

"Honey, would you come here, please? Kitty, here girl. Come here."

Hearing these words, I left my work in the kitchen and walked to the bedroom. Kitty, our little three-pound toy poodle, hopped off the couch where she had been sleeping and followed me into the bedroom. Kitty had been my husband's dog before we were married. He had trained her well; she always came immediately when he called her.

John, my husband, met us at the door and asked us both to take a seat on the bed. I sat down on the edge of the bed. Kitty hopped up on the bed and sat down right beside me. We both gave him our complete attention.

Just three months earlier, my husband and I had been married. We were newlyweds. We had met the previous year, fallen in love, and married, but learning to live with another person can be challenging. We lived in a small house with a tiny bedroom. Consequently, in order to have any space between our bed and our dresser, the bed was pushed up against a wall. The room was also adjacent to a small bathroom.

I had started a habit of walking out of the bathroom after a shower with a towel wrapped around my wet body and another one around my wet hair. Then, standing in front of the dresser and mirror, I'd unwrap the towel from around my hair and drop it on the bed as I began to brush my hair and blow it dry. The side of the bed which my wet towel always landed on happened to be John's side. Many nights he found himself crawling into a bed that was damp and cold.

John had asked me several times if I would please alter my routine such that my wet towel was not dropped on his side of the bed. But somehow, I never seemed to be able to remember his request. My actions were by no means intentional, but his bed ended up damp and cold just the same. Every time he said something to me about it, I responded with the good intentions to stop, but I had formed a habit, and a habit is hard to break.

So, there we were, Kitty and I, sitting in rapt attention on the edge of the bed, all four eyes on my husband. He moved from the door closer to us. Standing in front of the two of us, he began to speak.

"I am afraid I need to talk to the two of you about a serious matter," he said in a solemn tone of voice. "It has come to my attention that one of you has been leaving a wet towel on my side of the bed. Now, I don't know which one of you has been doing this . . . and I don't need to know." He continued earnestly, gesturing as he spoke. "I would just like the behavior to stop."

I chuckled as I began to apologize, but he waved me away saying, "Uh, uh. I don't need to hear any confessions from either one of you. In fact, it would probably be better if I never know which one is the guilty party. I would just like the behavior stopped, please."

I burst out laughing and kissed him on his

cheek. It was such an amusing way for him to get his point across. And it worked. Never again did I drop a wet towel on his side of the bed. From then on, every time I unwrapped my hair and started to drop my towel on the bed, I remembered my funny husband and chuckled as I walked to the bathroom to hang my towel on the towel rack.

That was many years ago. Like any couple we have had our ups and downs, but over forty years later, we still tease about that funny episode. Many times, through the years, we have told each other of some new negative behavior that we suspected Kitty may have been guilty of (or whatever other pet we had at the time). She has been suspected of many infractions such as leaving the cap off of the toothpaste, not cleaning water left on the sink, forgetting to leave phone messages, etc. Why, once she was even suspected of parking the car crooked in the garage, making it difficult for the other one of us to get the second car pulled into the garage.

I will always remember John's amusing way of getting me to change my behavior. Climbing into a cold, damp bed at night after a hard day's work was surely more than frustrating, especially after repeated requests for me to stop my offensive behavior. He could so easily have handled it with anger instead of humor. Keeping our sense of humor is healthy for us, according to the Bible—like good medicine.

**Prayer:** Heavenly Father, thank You for humor. And thank You for showing us that You smile at good humor, too. Help us to learn to laugh instead of other less helpful emotions. In Jesus' name, amen.

**Thought for the Day:** Try laughing at your circumstances instead of becoming frustrated or angry.

## Day 4: Seeking the Lost

by Harriet
Read Luke 15:4-7

*For the Son of Man came to seek and save the lost.*
Luke 19:10

We were experiencing a downpour outside. A cold front had moved in earlier that day, and that summer night was wet, cold, and miserable. The rain came down in sheets, blowing sideways at times and making sideways streaks against the street lamp at the corner of the block in my neighborhood . . . and my husband was out in the pouring rain trying to find our little dog. Kitty had been a terrific dog, but she had lived a long life and at the time of this storm, she had become quite old. Her eyes had grown dim and she had trouble seeing. Her hearing was not the best either, so she relied mostly on her sense of smell to find her way back home when we let her out. A downpour like we were experiencing rendered her sense of smell unreliable. Usually when we let her out in our unfenced backyard, she did her business and came right back inside. This night she did not, so my husband set out to find her.

"I can't find her," my distraught husband said as he stepped back inside, after being out for quite a while, water dripping off of him from all sides, his clothes soaked and clinging to him, in spite of the rain jacket he wore. "Honey, she's lost in all this rain. She can't smell her way back. If I don't find her, she might never find her way back. I have to go out again for a while longer. I can't give up on her yet," he said as he headed outside again.

I stood at the window straining to make out anything in the dark, outside world. It was mostly to no avail. I could see the rain streaking down our back window and the golden glow of the streetlight about a block away, but that was all. Finally, after a long time, John came back inside with our tiny, shivering, and very wet dog held in his arms, pulled close to his chest for warmth.

"Where did you find her?" I asked.

"Well," John replied, "I was about to give up but then thought to myself, if I were a dog who could not see well, where would I go? Then I looked around and our neighbor across the street has a very bright porch light on. So, I thought maybe Kitty could see that and would go toward the light. I walked over there, climbed the stairs to their front door, and there huddled against the door was Kitty."

Whenever I read the biblical passages about the Good Shepherd seeking out his lost sheep, this is the mental image that comes to my mind. I see the Good Shepherd as my sweet husband, so worried about the little dog he loves. I see him standing at my front door, cold and wet from being outside for more than an hour in a downpour; holding a shivering, old dog that had once been lost but now was found. How precious to imagine Jesus holding me—lost and dirty in my sins–but still held tight in His arms, close to His heart.

**Prayer:** Gracious Heavenly Father, thank You for seeking and finding me. Thank You for holding me close at times when I was lost and confused. In Jesus' name, amen.

**Thought for the Day:** When we were still lost in our sins, Christ loved us enough to die for us. He indeed came to seek and to save souls who were lost and doomed without Him.

## Day 5: Like Father, Like Son

by Harriet
Read John 6:46-51

*No one has ever seen God, but the one and only Son, who is himself God and is in closest relationship with the Father, has made him known.*
John 1:18 (NIV)

Our little three-pound toy poodle that my husband and I had at the beginning of our marriage, has been the inspiration for several of the previous devotions, but today, I will tell about two other dogs we have had and loved—Buckles and Colt. They were father and son, with Buckles being Colt's father.

Somewhere down the line, my husband John learned about English Field Cockers. He decided he wanted one at a time when our previous pet had passed away, and we were without a pet. No one bred or sold English Field Cockers in our city, so John drove several hours to purchase our dog. One of my sons fell in love with the dog and very much wanted one to call his own. He begged us for a pet of his own and willingly paid the two hundred dollars it cost. He was a teenager at the time and had the money from working during the summers, and he wore us down until we finally agreed.

John drove back to purchase another puppy. The breeder told him all he had was a rare brown and white puppy, the runt of the litter. My son didn't want to wait any longer, so my husband agreed to buy that one. We named him Buckles.

The first time I laid eyes on Buckles, I thought he was either the most beautiful puppy I had ever seen or the ugliest, and I really wasn't sure which it was. He was beautiful but at the same time sort of looked like a baby cow.

Buckles grew up to become absolutely gorgeous and possibly our favorite pet of all time. He was sweet, smart, obedient, and an overall wonderful pet. We loved our other English Cocker, but Buckles ended up just a little sweeter, a little more obedient, a little more lovable, and a lot smarter. We ended up paying my son back his two hundred dollars when he went to college, and we kept Buckles as our pet.

One of John's friends and hunting buddies loved Buckles, too, and he wanted one just like him. But, all the breeder had at the time was a solid black female dog which the friend bought and named Ziggy. After a few years, the friend wanted Ziggy to have puppies by Buckles, and though we had them together several times, she never conceived. Finally, when Buckles was about ten years old, the friend decided to seek help from a veterinarian and have Ziggy artificially inseminated. The procedure was successful, and Ziggy gave birth to six of Buckles's puppies—all either solid black or black and white, but not a brown one among them. We were given our pick of the litter.

Choosing our new puppy proved to be a challenge. We knew we wanted a puppy with the personality of Buckles, but which to choose? When they ran out to us, one of them, a fat little solid black guy, ran out wiggling from side to side like a slinky pet—the exact same funny disjointed run Buckles had. Then, when we picked this little guy up, he snuggled his nose into our necks and wagged his little tail happily, just like his dad. The other puppies did not do this.

Though we would have thought we would have wanted either a brown puppy, of which there were none, or at least the runt of the litter, we ended up choosing this fat, solid black puppy because he reminded us so much of Buckles, his dad, whom we knew well and loved with all our hearts.

Recognizing the son, Colt, because he bore the traits of his father reminds me of Jesus and His Heavenly Father. In Jesus' case, we have not seen the Father, but because Jesus lived and His life and ministry are recorded for us, we can look at Him and know what our Heavenly Father is like. Colossians 1:15 tells us that Jesus is the visible image of the invisible God.

**Prayer:** Thank You, God, for giving us Jesus so that we may know what You are like. We are Your children, too. Help us to be enough like You that others can see Jesus in us. In Jesus' name, amen.

**Thought for the Day:** Are you and I enough like our Heavenly Father that others can learn what He is like by getting to know us?

Chapter 8

# Where It's Summer All Year

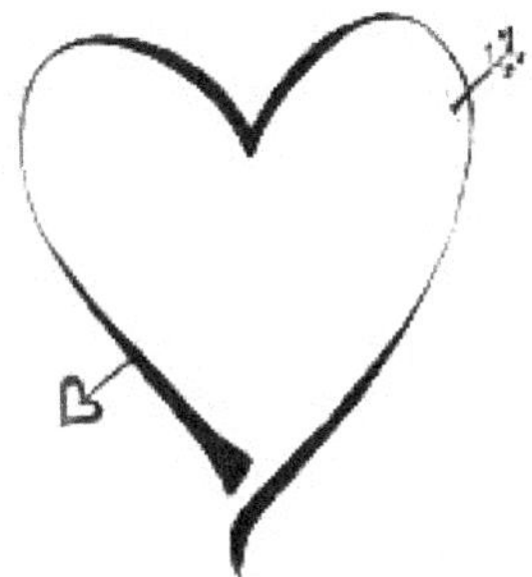

## Day 1: Parched Places

by Harriet
Read Isaiah 58:10-12

*The LORD will guide you always; he will satisfy your needs in a sun-scorched land . . . You will be like a well-watered garden, like a spring whose waters never fail.*
Isaiah 58:11 (NIV)

As most of our readers know by now, Shirley and I grew up in Nigeria, a country on the west coast of Africa. It is hot year-round in Nigeria and similar tropical places. When we came to this point in our year-long devotional series, this book dedicated to the summer season, we could not resist writing an entire chapter where the devotions are all derived from inspirations from our childhood—the things that we grew up accustomed to seeing and experiencing in that land where it is summer all year long.

Nigeria, like so many other tropical nations, has only two seasons—one that is filled with predominantly rainy days and the other that can be quite dry. These seasons are simply called the rainy season and the dry season. During the rainy season, it rains at least a little while every day for six months. The world greens up, trees bear fruit, and gardens flourish. But during the dry season, we wouldn't get any rain at all for the other six months of the year and boy, could things get dry. Plants dried up, the ground became barren and dusty, and the trees and plants that still had leaves on them became brown with dust.

I used to love to play outdoors and like all children, I played hard. Because the weather was warm, even hot, all the time, I played outside most every day. Our reading passage speaks of a sun-scorched land in verse 11. I can well remember what a sun-scorched land was like. I remember how thirsty I would get playing in such a land in the middle of the dry season. Back then, we had a filter only on the faucet in the kitchen so that was the only faucet from which we could safely drink the water. We had an outside spigot, but it did not have a filter. It was for watering the garden only. I usually didn't want to stop my play to go back inside for a drink of water, so I'd wait as long as I could. I can remember being really hot and thirsty as I ran inside to get a glass of clean, refreshing, safe water to drink.

Today's verse brings these images to my mind as it draws the contrast between the sun-scorched land and a fresh, pure spring whose waters never fail. Isn't that a wonderful promise from God? But God doesn't make this promise in a void. A thorough reading of today's passage will reveal a connection of God's promise to satisfy us in difficult times with our willingness to show kindness to others. Verse 10 says, ". . . if you will spend yourselves in behalf of the hungry and satisfy the needs of the oppressed. . . ."

May we always be mindful that God notices when we show kindness to His other children and that He rewards us. He guides us and satisfies our needs, even in a sun-scorched land.

**Prayer:** Gracious Heavenly Father, thank You for Your love and faithfulness. Thank You for taking note when we show kindness to others and for repaying us with blessings. Your word is full of kind promises to us. In Jesus' name, amen.

**Thought for the Day:** God notices and rewards us when we show kindness to others. He transcends our circumstances and repays us with blessings from above.

## Day 2: Summer in My Heart

by Shirley
Read Romans 8:24-28

*Set your minds on things that are above,*
*not on things that are on earth.*
*Colossians 3:2*

One very cold winter morning when we lived in Gadsden, Alabama, I went to pick up my big brother Paul to take him to work since his van was broken down. On our way to the construction site where he was working, I asked Paul how he could stand to work outside in the freezing weather. He said he had layers of sweaters and jackets, very heavy socks and work boots, and heavy gloves to wear. Just about then, we arrived at the site and he got out of the car and grabbed his coffee thermos and lunch bag. He leaned back into the car and said, "In my heart, I'm in Nigeria, so it's summer in my heart."

Paul expressed the sentiment of many of the

Nigeria missionary kids (MKs) I know. One of my Nigeria missionary aunts used to say, "Thankfully, God will always inhabit my heart that holds a Nigeria-shaped vault." She meant that her heart would always hold dear her Nigerian people, Nigeria missionaries, and all the experiences she had while serving there.

We hold in our hearts memories of the Nigerian people, our friends who were part of our family. We remember the fun times we shared as well as the difficulties we shared. We hold dear our Nigeria mission family and remember all the outrageous things that happened to us while we lived there. We remember the year-round warm weather that allowed us to play outdoors almost every day, even during the rainy season. Many times, when Mom would call us to come in for supper we would have to stand in the yard and get all the mud and dirt hosed off of us before we could go inside and get really cleaned up.

We had a variety of pets, including dogs, cats, lizards, snakes of all sorts, spiders, monkeys, baboons, parrots, birds, and just about any other animal you could think of. We could walk into our yard and pick fruit off the tree and eat it right on the spot. When I bite into a guava and close my eyes, I can see the guava trees on the hospital compound. We shared all of our toys with each other.

I also have summer in my heart as I am comforted by such precious memories. As Christ-followers, we can always have summer in our hearts since the Holy Spirit dwells in us.

Summer usually offers opportunities to spend more time with family and friends and take vacation trips to the beach or mountains. If you have children or grandchildren, your summers are likely filled with taking them to swim, to sports practices, and to various activities.

What is supposed to be a more leisurely, restful season of the year gets hectic and our schedules are jam-packed every day of the week. If we aren't careful in protecting our time with the Lord—personally and corporately—that time can easily get squeezed out and left behind.

We get so busy with everything that we skip our Bible reading, studying, memorizing, contemplating, and meditating, and spending time with the Lord in prayer. This results in our not being interested in the things of God and in worshiping Him. All of these things dim the summer in our hearts.

We must make certain that we guard our time in "seeking the things above" (Colossians 3:1). As a result, Jesus Christ becomes the center and focus of all our summer activities and brings us refreshment, rest, and security.

We have summer in our hearts when the light of Jesus Christ shines in and through us. It saves, gives rest, refreshes, strengthens, and gives security as it compels and propels us to share the gospel with all those with whom we come in contact.

**Prayer:** Heavenly Father, thank You for the light of Jesus Christ that gives us summer in our hearts. In the busyness of our days, may we be diligent to guard our time with You so that our relationship with You remains unhindered. In Jesus' name, amen.

**Thought for the Day:** What things are you allowing to diminish the summer in your heart?

## Day 3: What's in a Name?

by Harriet
Read Philippians 2:8-11

*For to us a child is born, to us a son is given; and the government shall be upon his shoulder, and his name shall be called Wonderful Counselor, Mighty God, Everlasting Father, Prince of Peace.*
Isaiah 9:6

What's in a name?

Have you ever thought much about names? Why were you given your name by your parents? Why did you name your own children as you did?

In my family, the parents named the children with names of ancestry, passing down family names from generation to generation. We modified this a bit with our only daughter, giving her a middle name after my mother-in-law, but assigning a favorite girl's name that wasn't part of our lineage as her first name. (Just so you have the connections, this is the illustrator of this book, Kristen Conant Michael.)

While we had a tradition for the naming of our

children, I never looked into the meanings of the names we gave them. Not like names are chosen in some countries.

In Nigeria, for example, names usually have a deeper meaning. When I was a child, there, I lived among the Yoruba people. I learned about the name meanings when our Nigerian friends bestowed names upon my siblings and me. My older brother, the oldest of my parents' four children, was given the name Bankole, which means "build a house with me." This name is often given to first children, especially first sons. I was given the name Bamidele, which translates to mean "come home with me." The name was given to me because I was the only child in my family to be born overseas. This name is commonly given to children, like me, who were born in a country other than their parents' homeland. Many of my missionary-kid friends were given this name by the Nigerians, too, since many of them were also born there. My older sister's name struck us all as funny. She was called Kikalama which means "the one to be spoiled," or in other words the child who demanded the most attention. Our Nigerian friends had observed us well. Her name still makes me chuckle. And my younger sister, the baby of the family, was called Ayodele, which means "joy comes to the home," and is often given to a youngest, bonus child.

Jesus, too, has a meaningful name, given to Him by God; several names, actually. The name Jesus was given to Mary by the angel Gabriel. It means "the one who saves." He was also called Emmanuel in Matthew 1:23, which means "God with us." Our passage today gives several other names for Jesus as well—Wonderful Counselor, Mighty God, Everlasting Father, and Prince of Peace.

Our passage also tells us that Jesus' name will be exalted above all other names and that at His name, every knee will bow, and every mouth will confess that He is Lord.

**Prayer:** Heavenly Father, like my friends in Nigeria, names have meanings to You. Your names as listed in so many places in the Scripture each represent an aspect of who You are. And, Jesus' names too, are rich in meaning. Teach us to appreciate the names taught in Your word for You and for Jesus, Your Son, in whose name we pray, amen.

**Thought for the Day:** As a Christ-follower, when people refer to you as a Christian, you are bearing Christ's name in that term. Let's live in a manner worthy of His great name.

## Day 4: This is Not Home

by Shirley
Read 1 Peter 1:1-12

*But our citizenship is in heaven,*
*and from it we await a Savior, the Lord Jesus Christ,*
*who will transform our lowly body*
*to be like his glorious body,*
*by the power that enables him even*
*to subject all things to himself.*
Philippians 3:20-21

"Can you believe she hasn't ever had snow ice cream?" a girl who lived a couple of doors down from us asked another friend my first winter in the States when we received several inches of snow in Birmingham, Alabama.

"Well, no," I said "Before now I have only seen snow in pictures and heard about snow ice cream."

As you read, keep in mind that we were in Nigeria decades before Internet and cell phones could be found in even remote villages as they are today. It took six weeks for a telegram to go from

Nigeria to the States and vice versa. Missionaries and missionary kids couldn't easily jump on a plane and get back to the States quickly when a family member was seriously ill or had died.

Harriet and I grew up where it was always summer. Our experiences in our adopted homeland, Nigeria, were vastly different from other children our age who grew up in the States. Sometimes, that made me feel left out as other children laughed at things I had never heard about or didn't know how to do. Although missionaries referred to the United States as "home," I told my parents, "This is not home."

Thankfully, my older siblings and parents helped me understand that we experienced many things in Nigeria that those children who grew up in Birmingham had never heard about unless it was in school, a magazine, or a movie.

From then on, when others would make fun of me for not knowing about something all the other children knew about, my feelings wouldn't get hurt and I wouldn't feel left out. In fact, I felt sorry for those children who did not get to experience all the things we did.

Most of the children in Birmingham didn't have pet monkeys and baboons. They didn't get invited into a king's court. They didn't get to watch Nigerian goldsmiths at work as they took raw gold nuggets and melted them so the impurities would rise to the top, get skimmed off, and produce gold so pure and soft that American jewelers wouldn't want to work with it. They didn't get to visit leprosy colonies and remote villages hidden deep in the African jungle. They likely didn't get to watch surgeries and babies being born at the hospital. They didn't have to chase those large orange lizards out from under their bed covers before crawling in. They may have never slept under a mosquito net. They never watched the *Egunguns* (Yoruba masked/costumed people) dance. They didn't get to watch the weavers as they produced their beautifully colored material. They never heard the talking drums. They didn't know how to tie a baby on their backs and carry him or her around all day. They couldn't speak or understand Pidgin, Yoruba, or Hausa. They didn't get to eat pounded yam, *egusi* soup, *akara*, *chin-chin*, curried chicken/groundnut stew, python, or lizard. They didn't get to see the most beautiful sunrises and sunsets anywhere in the world. They never witnessed the joyful dancing nor heard the beautiful music and singing in Hausa and Yoruba.

You see, as strange as Birmingham and the things to which I was being introduced were to me, Nigeria and the things I knew about were strange to them.

Regardless of whether we call Nigeria, Alabama, or anywhere else home, as Christ-followers this world is not home, heaven is.

Today's Scripture reading in 1 Peter tells us:

- We are "born again to a living hope" (1:3).
- We are chosen before the world began (1:2).
- We are "elect exiles" scattered all over (1:1).
- We live now and for eternity because of Jesus Christ (1:3).
- We are satisfied with our eternal inheritance (1:4-5).
- We will experience trials and sorrows in

this world (1:6-7).

- We have salvation that will save us from this world (1:7-9).

As Christ-followers, we live in a foreign land—the world—as we serve God using our unique mix of God-given gifts, talents, and abilities we are to exercise as we serve Him.

We are reminded in today's key passage that regardless of the uncertainties and circumstances that surround us, we have the assurance that God is in control and we are citizens of heaven. That truth gives us comfort, strength, and stamina as we pass through this place to our eternal home.

**Prayer:** Heavenly Father, thank You that through the sacrifice of Jesus Christ we are Your people and that You will be with us through whatever circumstances we face on this earth and bring us into our eternal homes in heaven when our lives here on earth are ended. In Jesus' name, amen.

**Thought for the Day:** Since we are God's people and this place is not our home, we can walk through any circumstance with the knowledge that our eternal home is prepared for our arrival.

## Day 5: Our Great God

by Harriet
Read 1 John 4:1-6

*Little children, you are from God . . . He who is in you is greater than he who is in the world.*
1 John 4:4 (NASB)

My house in Ogbomoso, Nigeria, was located on the hospital compound, since both of my parents worked in the hospital. My physician father held clinics and performed surgeries and deliveries, and my nurse mother worked in the operating room as the nurse supervisor.

The homes in this compound were all located just behind the hospital. A dirt road behind the hospital sloped down a small hill with about a half dozen homes sitting on either side of it. Our home was situated on the side of that road closest to the hospital and was well within walking distance of the hospital. In fact, a little dirt path cut through the property just behind our lot and led directly to the hospital. My dad owned a bicycle and would sometimes take it to the hospital, if called in suddenly, and on clear days, my parents often walked together to and from work. They had a car, too, which they could use if the weather warranted it.

One evening as they approached our house while walking home after a long day's work, my father spied something on our front steps. He stopped in his tracks and put out his arm to block my mom's forward progression as he told my mother to stop as well. Then Mom saw it too. There before them on the top step lay *juju*—the Nigerian form of a curse.

The juju on our steps consisted of some African beads along with the bones of a small animal mixed in a clod of dirt with blood, feathers, and feces. My parents recognized it as juju, immediately. Someone had placed a curse on our home.

The juju gave my father pause. He knew it had been placed as a curse, and this was cause for concern. But as he stood still, pondering the situation, my mother took a step forward. Then she walked right up the steps until she stood by the juju and without hesitation, she kicked it hard—right off of our front steps. The juju broke into pieces as it hit the ground below.

My father was taken aback by Mom's actions. Didn't she take this seriously? Didn't she know someone had tried to invoke demonic spirts to harm us when whoever it was had placed this juju there?

Mom never wavered. She looked my dad directly in the eyes and said emphatically, "Greater is He who is in me than he who is in the world. Because of Jesus' blood shed on the cross for me, I can kick juju right off of my doorstep!"

In an instant, my dad knew Mom was right. She had spoken an eternal truth.

Our God is an awesome God. He has overcome the enemy. He defeated Satan and all his minions at the cross. Because of that eternal truth, we who believe in Jesus as our Savior can kick juju off of our doorsteps. We can handle whatever other challenges we may face, too, because, as my mother so correctly stated, "Greater is He who is in us than he who is in the world."

**Prayer:** Father, we confess that Jesus is the Christ. We thank You, Father, for overcoming the world through Jesus' death and resurrection. Make us cognizant of the truth that Your Spirit in us is greater than anything the enemy of our souls, who is in the world, can throw at us. In Jesus' name, amen.

**Thought for the Day**: Through Jesus Christ whose Spirit dwells in believers, we are more than conquerors.

Chapter 9

# Mission Trips and Other Summer Things

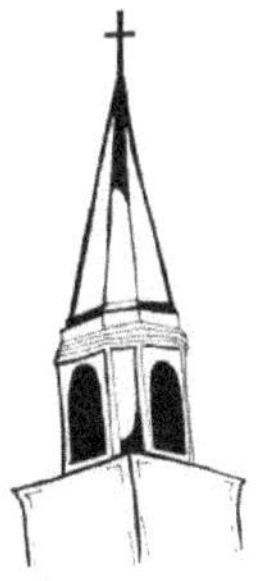

## Day 1: A Church Full of Missionaries

by Shirley
Read Mark 6:14-20

*And he said to them, "Go into all the world and proclaim the gospel to the whole creation."*
Mark 16:15

Summer is a great time for participating in mission trips and in-depth disciple-making. When I made that statement in a conversation with several people at a conference, one of the ladies told me she didn't have the gift of evangelism and that God had not called her to be a missionary.

I told her about when I lived in Atlanta, Georgia. I had gone to lunch one day after church with two church friends and a couple who had visited in our service that morning.

After we ordered our meal, I asked one of the young men from church to tell the new couple a little about himself. He started with, "The most exciting thing you need to know about me is what God did in my life, the lives of other team members who were in Brazil, and the Brazilian people during our trip." He proceeded to tell how God had convicted him of his sins of materialism and pride. He talked about the Lord giving him the courage to talk through an interpreter, with total strangers, about Jesus, and about how the Lord had convicted him that he didn't have to go to Brazil to share the gospel message.

The new young lady asked the lady from my church what drew her to the church. She said, "The truth of God's word is taught, and they understand that every person is to be equipped and taught to evangelize and disciple others."

The new man asked me with what in the church I was involved. I told him, "I sing in the adult choir, lead the preschool choir, and am on the missions committee."

He said, "Why is missions such a big deal?"

The young man from my church said, "Her parents were missionaries, so she didn't have much of a choice."

I took a few seconds to formulate my thoughts and then explained that just because someone is a missionary kid does not mean they will have a passion for missions. I also explained that my real passion is to make disciple-makers, and that's what missions is all about.

Our food came, and that train of discussion dropped off. After we started eating, I asked the couples to tell us a little about themselves. They were from the Midwest and had moved to the Atlanta metropolitan area for her husband to work for the Centers for Disease Control. She was raised going to church; he wasn't.

I asked what had brought them to our church that morning and found out they had been driving around looking at homes and pulled into the church parking lot to look at their map (obviously this was before everyone had GPS). The lady who placed fresh flowers in the sanctuary each week was leaving the church and saw them sitting in the car. She and her husband circled around and asked if they needed any help.

The younger couple told them the street name they were looking for. The church member told them it was a little difficult to find and offered to lead them where they were going. When they got to the house, the church members got out of their car and introduced themselves to the younger couple. The man mentioned that he wasn't sure this house was in the best neighborhood for a young couple, because there was a news report of a shooting or robbery in that area almost every night.

The couple had apparently been looking for a while and were disappointed not to have found anything. The church couple asked the younger couple if they would like to join them for lunch and suggested the younger couple follow them to the restaurant.

After ordering, the couples began talking and finding out about each other. Not too far into the conversation, the church lady invited the younger couple to come to church the next Sunday and meet some of the church family.

Apparently by the way the couple stumbled to answer them, the church man realized they did not attend church. The church man said, "Even if you haven't been to church before, come and meet our church family and make a few friends. We won't be there because we'll be at another church celebrating our grandson's baptism."

The new wife replied that they weren't really

church people, even though she had been a member at a church back home, to which the church wife replied, “Neither are we. We love Jesus and people and love to hear the Bible preached and taught.”

The young woman continued, "We showed up. Several people greeted us in the parking lot, and when we walked into the church a man came over and asked our names and said that the couple who led us to that house had told him to be on the lookout for us, and he invited us to sit with him and his family."

She stopped telling her story. I was about to say something, and she continued, “I think your church must be full of missionaries, because everyone I met wanted to know if I have a relationship with Jesus.”

You know what? I think she was right. While the Lord calls some to tell people about Jesus in specific places through specific ministries, The Great Commission tells us that as we go about doing the things the Lord has called us to do in the places he calls us to do them, we are to make disciple-makers.

All Christ-followers are to be disciple-makers

and missionaries. We are to be sharing the gospel with unbelievers so that they might come to a saving knowledge of Jesus. We are also to share the gospel with believers so they will be encouraged and taught and become stronger witnesses for the Lord.

When people meet you and spend time around you, do they see you as a missionary or disciple-maker?

**Prayer:** Heavenly Father, thank You for the faithful men and women throughout the ages who have served You as missionaries and disciple-makers all over the world. Help us know You better and give us a passion to share the gospel with others. In Jesus' name, amen.

**Thought for the Day:** As you walk through your day, look for opportunities to share the gospel with those whom the Lord brings across your path.

## Day 2: Special

by Harriet
Read Zechariah 14:20-21

*He has made everything beautiful in its time.*
*He has also set eternity in the human heart;*
*yet no one can fathom what God has done*
*from beginning to end.*
Ecclesiastes 3:11

"Special" read the large sign taped to the side of a bus which sat in a used vehicle lot in Tegucigalpa, Honduras. The students on the mission trip the year the bus was purchased chose to name the bus "Special" after the mission team bought it for the church in La Paz with whom they had worked many summers. They said the sign on its side may have been there to advertise a special sale on that particular bus, but they thought it made a perfect name for her as well.

A few years ago, I had the privilege of participating in this annual student trip as a chaperone. The students on the trip came from the

Christian school where two of my children graduated and where I have worked as a substitute teacher for over fifteen years. I have a degree in nursing, even though I no longer work in that field. I found that working part-time as a substitute allowed me more time to write while also keeping me in touch with my children who attended the school. But that year, they needed a nurse to go along on the trip, so they asked me. Growing up on the mission field, I eagerly said yes to their request.

Having now spent time in Special, I can vouch for the fact that she was well named. She had a cracked windshield that could not be replaced because a piece of glass with the correct dimensions was all but impossible to find in Honduras, and having it shipped there would have been too costly, so the church just drove her anyway—cracked windshield and all. Sometimes Special developed other problems which needed attention. The week I was there, she broke down altogether when the church was driving our mission team back across the mountain to Tegucigalpa to catch our return flight home. Fortunately, we had put a day of shopping and sight-seeing into our schedule, so sitting on the side of the road for several hours while men from the church first tried to fix the problem and then arranged for another bus to come pick us up and take us the rest of the way did not cause us to miss our flight.

In spite of her tendency to develop problems, Special faithfully went up and down winding, mountainous roads every week to bring people to church who would otherwise not have been able to worship. I thought we were going to flip over or slide down the side of a steep hill more than once when I was in Special. But I also saw the smiling faces of happy children run to the bus to be taken to the church from some of the poorest homes I have ever seen.

Zechariah 14:20-21 speaks of the holiness of even the cups and cooking pots in the temple. Indeed, God's purpose for all things is their holiness. I suppose if cups and cooking pots can be special to the Lord, then so can an old bus with a cracked windshield.

God's people are a bit like that, too. God's purpose for us is our holiness, and we are all special in our own ways. God created us differently for His unique purposes. He loves our specialness, and He has placed eternity in our hearts.

**Prayer:** Heavenly Father, thank You for the uniqueness of Your plan for each of our lives. Help us to appreciate our own specialness and that of others. In Jesus' name, amen.

**Thought for the day:** God makes everything beautiful in its time.

## Day 3: Vacation Bible School

by Shirley

Read Psalm 78:1-8

*We will not hide them from their children,*
*but tell to the coming generation*
*the glorious deeds of the LORD, and his might,*
*and the wonders that he has done.*
Psalm 78:4

Some of my fondest memories of summer are of Vacation Bible Schools (VBS) from my childhood, teen, and adult years. There are only a few years scattered throughout that I have not been involved in VBS as a student, helper, or teacher.

I remember the excitement of lining up and marching into the opening assembly. We did the pledges to the American and Christian flags and the Bible, learned our Scripture memory verse, and sang songs. Granted, in the olden days when I was a child, the stage decorations weren't as elaborate as they are now, yet we still learned the lessons and themes.

If you had asked me when I was a child what I liked best about VBS, I would have said the music. The songs were always easy to learn and fun to sing, but more importantly we got to do movements and dance around while we sang songs like, "Jesus Loves the Little Children," "This Little Light of Mine," "Jesus Loves Me," "I've Got the Joy, Joy, Joy, Joy, Down in My Heart," and "Deep and Wide." Then, there were always songs that reinforced the Bible verses we were learning and the Bible stories we heard.

There were always those wonderfully creative and fun men and women who dressed up in silly costumes, danced, and sang. They found unique ways to present biblical truth to us. The children had opportunities to play parts in dramas which helped reinforce biblical truth. I can still remember when I was ten or eleven, I was assigned the part of the one sheep that wandered away from the rest of the herd. The script for the drama had the other sheep talking about how the shepherd shouldn't bother going after that one crazy sheep. Instead, he should stay there and tend to those who had not strayed.

One of the wise old sheep asked these younger sheep a question. “If you wandered off and got lost, would you want the shepherd to come look for you?” They all agreed they would. Then, the older sheep explained that God seeks out people who are lost and go astray. That biblical truth is indelibly burned in my mind, and thankfully in time, God sought to bring me (a lost sheep) into His fold as I came to know Him as my Savior.

We would all sit around a table and be served Kool-Aid in a little paper cup and two cookies on a napkin. Yummy.

What I didn’t realize when I was a child but began to grasp as a teenager and later an adult, is that through these songs, the truths of the Bible were being planted in my heart. Dr. Bryan Chapell says that the first theology lesson most of us learn is from “Jesus Loves Me.” This simple hymn, in just the first verse, reminds us that Jesus loves us and that the authority on that is the Bible.

All of these songs helped me understand that God is Creator, Savior, Sustainer, and Lord. I learned that the Bible is God’s very word and it is true. I learned that everything I needed to know about how to live a life that pleases God is found in His word. I learned that God commanded me to share His love and truth with all those whom He brings across my path. Each part of VBS, including crafts and recreation— reinforced the biblical truths in our memory verse and Bible studies. Little did I realize that I was not only learning biblical truth, I was also learning how to teach that truth to others.

As a teenager, I was a helper in VBS. My first year, I was very excited to be able to help teach children what I knew about Jesus. But, in retrospect, those VBS interactions were more about teaching me than my teaching children, as I learned not only how to teach the truth of God's word, but how to live out His commands.

As an adult I have loved watching children of all ages begin to grasp the truth of God's word and His love for them. I have also learned much about God and how to teach and share His love with children. I have had the privilege of walking alongside children as they came to know Jesus as their Savior and Lord. What a joy to see excited children quoting Scripture and telling Bible stories to their parents, many of whom were not Christ-followers.

One church in which I was involved had numerous parents come with their children, and they wanted to know about Jesus, so we switched gears a bit and added an adult VBS class.

I know some churches are very small and may not be able to do a VBS on their own. If that's the case for you, find ways to join with other churches in your area for a multi-church or community VBS.

**Prayer:** Heavenly Father, thank You for the countless Christ-following men and women who have served You through VBS. Give us a passion to serve in our church or community VBS so that seeds of the truths of Your word are planted and fed, and so those children may come to know You as their Savior and Lord. In Jesus' name, amen.

**Thought for the Day:** Is God calling you to be one of those wonderfully creative and fun men or women who dress up in silly costumes, dance, and sing while teaching the truths of God's word and loving children?

## Day 4: Suffering and Glory

by Harriet
Read 1 Peter 1:3-12

*Inquiring what person or time the Spirit of Christ in them was indicating when he predicted the sufferings of Christ and the subsequent glories . . .*
*things into which angels long to look.*
1 Peter 1:11-12b

The man's eyes filled with tears as the students began to wash his feet. The man, a member of a remote village in Honduras, had traveled miles and waited for hours in order to see a doctor at the clinic that day. Finally, he was able to see the visiting American doctor who had come on this short-term mission trip sponsored by a Christian high school.

The man had a disfiguring disease. Working as a nurse at that clinic, I saw patients first and often was able treat them with nursing care or simple skin creams or antibiotics in the case of ear infections. But, I took one look at this man and knew his problem was more than I could handle, so I directed him to the doctor's station. His skin was pulled taut across his face, distorting his features. He almost looked like he had suffered major burns. As it turned out, his skin had this same taut, scarred look all over his body. And the man said that his skin hurt, all the time.

The doctor knew immediately what was wrong with the man and was able to secure some soothing ointments as well as a referral to a medical center in Tegucigalpa, the capital of Honduras. Then, the man visited the last station of the clinic—the foot washing station.

Some of the students on the mission trip placed his feet in a bowl of clean, warm water and started gently washing them . . . and the man began to softly cry. He was not accustomed to people willingly standing near him, much less touching and washing his feet.

I learned later that this man had a sister with the same condition, and they both received helpful treatment at the medical center with our school paying for their care.

Suffering, glory, and faith tested by fire—these are the beauties on which angels long to look. And, these marvels are woven through the stories of human suffering. Stories of believers who have faced great difficulties while holding fast to their faith; a faith which is to them more precious than gold. Stories of believers who hold on to hope through the resurrection of Jesus Christ until at last, they obtain an eternal, imperishable and perfect inheritance.

What makes these stories so beautiful and so marvelous that they attract the eyes of angels? These stories of human suffering mixed with faith, hope, and eternal glory reflect the sufferings of Christ and the glory that followed. They are marvelous, indeed.

Have you ever thought about that? Have you ever found yourself tested by fire? Maybe you don't have a disfiguring skin disease that pulls your skin taut and causes it to hurt, but maybe you do have some other painful physical illness or affliction. Or, maybe you are being opposed, harassed, or are suffering emotionally in some way. Perhaps you have felt at times that your suffering was more than you could handle.

In times like these, remember, you are

reflecting the sufferings of your Lord. And it is something so beautiful and so amazing that even angels long to glimpse it. This, then, is reason to praise and honor Him who suffered for you; He whom you have loved even though you have never seen—proof of your faith. Rejoice in the privilege God has given you to join in His sufferings and reflect His glory. Remember, angels are watching.

**Prayer:** Thank You, Lord, for suffering for me on the cross. And thank You for suffering with me when I suffer. May I reflect Your glory in my suffering and may it be something so beautiful as to attract the eyes of angels. In Jesus' name, amen.

**Thought for the Day:** What sort of challenges, difficulties, or sufferings have you experienced? Did you know you were reflecting Christ's sufferings?

## Day 5: Withstanding the Heat

by Shirley
Read Daniel 3:16-30

*The hair of their heads was not singed,*
*their cloaks were not harmed,*
*and no smell of fire had come upon them.*
Daniel 3:27b

During summer, the temperatures rise to their highest level of the year. The heat creates a great environment in which to enjoy summer activities such as swimming and cooking out. Rainfall may increase during summer, increasing the humidity. The heat plus humidity can absolutely drain you of all energy and make you cranky.

Extremely hot conditions can cause big problems for people, animals, and plants, and sometimes droughts occur. There may be severe thunderstorms, gardens that die, and numerous wildfires.

In our spiritual summers, our lives seem somewhat stable, yet periods of spiritual challenges (extreme heat and storms) come from time to time. These challenges can strengthen our spiritual lives.

God promises to be with us during the storms and fires in our lives. God uses these storms and fires to strengthen our faith and trust in Him. When we come through the storms and fires, we are likely better able to appreciate the calmness of the weather afterward.

In today's passage, we read about Shadrach, Meshach, and Abednego being faithful to God as they refused to bow down to the statue of King Nebuchadnezzar. They were brought before the king who asked them, ". . . who is the god who will deliver you out of my hands?" (Daniel 3:15).

The men answered by saying "God whom we serve is able to deliver us from the burning fiery furnace, and he will deliver us out of your hand, O king" (Daniel 3:17). They further demonstrated their faith in God by saying that if God did not deliver them from the fire, "be it known to you, O king, that we will not serve your gods or worship the golden image that you have set up" (Daniel 3:18).

This response infuriated the king, who ordered

the soldiers to carry out a death sentence by binding the three men and throwing them into the fiery furnace that had been heated to seven times what they normally heated it. It was so hot that the flames killed those who were taking the men to the furnace.

Then King Nebuchadnezzar went and peeked in near the door of the furnace and was astonished to see four unbound men walking through the fire and not being burned by it. The king called Shadrach, Meshach, and Abednego to come out of the furnace, recognizing that they were "servants of the Most High God" (Daniel 3:26). The king decreed that no one could speak against "the God of Shadrach, Meshach, and Abednego," and the three men were promoted (Daniel 3:29-30).

While it is improbable that you or I will face being thrown into an actual fiery furnace, we will most certainly face fiery trials (1 Peter 4:12-13). We must prepare ourselves to stand firm during the fiery trials that come into our lives by diligently reading, studying, memorizing, contemplating, and meditating upon God's word. That way, we come to know Him and His character as we walk in obedience to His commands. Our faith in God is strengthened, enabling us to trust Him so that we are able to say, along with Shadrach, Meshach, and Abednego, "God is able and will deliver us." Furthermore, we are able to say with just as much certainty, "But if God chooses not to deliver us, we will not dishonor and disobey Him by worshiping your idols."

We need to pray that God would refine us like gold is refined by turning up the heat so that the impurities (sin) in our hearts would be recognized as sin against holy God. Then, we need to be quick to confess, repent of that sin, and walk in the freedom of God's forgiveness.

The Lord works in and through the circumstances of our lives, often "turning up the heat" so our faith in Him can be strengthened.

**Prayer:** Heavenly Father, thank You for "turning up the heat" in our lives so that we can be refined and made pure. Strengthen our faith so that we can withstand the fiery trials and so that You will be glorified. In Jesus' name, amen.

**Thought for the Day:** God is with you and will give you the mercy, grace, and strength you need to face the heat of your trials.

Chapter 10

# Spiders and Snakes

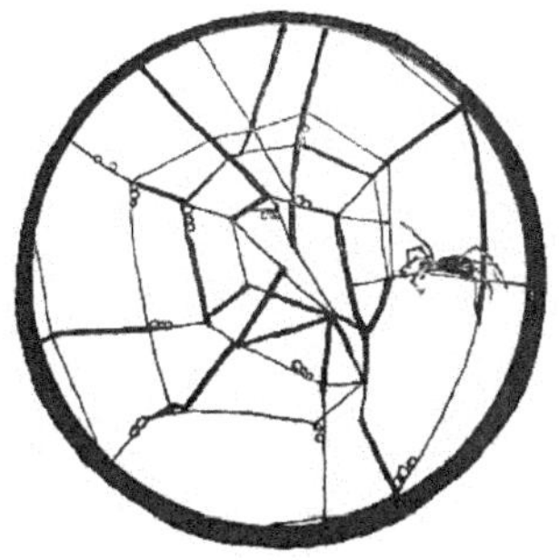

## Day 1: Snake on the Shelf

by Shirley
Read Genesis 3:1-24

*Then the LORD God said to the woman,*
*"What is this that you have done?"*
*The woman said, "The serpent deceived me, and I ate."*
Genesis 3:13

In today's passage, we read the account of Adam and Eve committing their first sin. Before this incident, they had lived sinless lives in close communion with God. Now, for the very first time since God created man, God's status, authority, and words were challenged, by the evil one and by Eve.

The serpent was used as an instrument of the evil one to deceive Eve. Chuck Smith gives us insight here. "Look how Satan hit her with a three-pronged attack. Lust of the flesh: it was good to eat. The lust of the eye: it was pleasant to behold. The pride of life: a tree designed to make one as wise as God." Then, she gave the fruit to Adam, and he ate it.

In Genesis 3:12, we see the first instance of blame-shifting when Adam tells God, “The woman whom you gave to be with me, she gave me fruit of the tree, and I ate.” Then Eve blames the serpent. That sounds a lot like us, doesn’t it? We don’t want to take responsibility for the sin we commit; we want it to be someone else’s fault.

As a counselor, sometimes I work with counselees who are processing how they are responsible for their sin. One thing I do is to have them look at the situation and determine which decisions they made at each juncture in the process. Next, we look at how they could have responded in a way that honored God.

Looking at this exchange between Eve and the serpent, we see numerous places where Eve could have responded in a way that honored God. We don’t “fall” into sin, we make choices along the way to succumb to temptation, and we choose to sin.

The sin committed by Adam and Eve was heinous and a willful act of disobedience to God that brought eternal separation from God. He cannot tolerate or condone sin.

Thankfully in Genesis 3:15, God gives us hope with the first proclamation of the gospel. We learn throughout Scripture that the shed blood of Jesus Christ is the only way for our sin to be forgiven, and the chasm between us and God to be closed so our relationship to Him can be restored. As we turn to Jesus in saving faith, death and sin no longer have a grip on us; we are set free.

Back in the garden, and now in our own lives, the evil one tempts us to doubt the truth of God's word. Our own sinful desires woo us. The world tempts us to follow its ways rather than God's.

Some spot it instantly, others take a while to spot it, and some never spot it. What is it? It is a three-foot green rubber snake, with its red forked tongue sticking out of its mouth. Its home is on the bookshelf in my office. It is coiled on a shelf with its head slithering down and onto the books below. Those books are written specifically for women and deal with issues that women face. I have the snake there to remind me of how easily the serpent deceived and misled Eve and how easily Eve succumbed to that temptation and sinned.

Each time I see that snake, I am reminded of

how easily I am deceived and misled by the evil one, my own sinful desires, and the temptations of the world. When I focus on the red forked tongue sticking out, I remember that my own words can mislead and tear down others.

**Prayer:** Heavenly Father, thank You that through Jesus You provided a way for our sin to be forgiven. We need You to help us not fall prey to the lies of the evil one, our own sinful desires, or the temptations of the world. Teach us to love and trust You more so that in those times of temptation, we can withstand the attacks and be Your faithful and obedient followers. In Jesus' name, amen.

**Thought for the Day:** Prepare yourself and be ready at any moment to withstand the temptations that lure you into sin.

## Day 2: Snake Stories

by Harriet
Read Genesis 3:1-7, 14-15

*The LORD God said to the serpent,*
*"Because you have done this, cursed are you above all livestock ... and on your belly you shall go and dust you shall eat all the days of your life. . . ."*
Genesis 3:14

Are you afraid of snakes? I sure am. My fear comes from my childhood in Nigeria where most of the snakes I could possibly have encountered were poisonous. Fortunately, I did not encounter many, though I do recall stumbling upon a few. One Sunday morning as we left for church, my mom spotted a baby cobra crawling out from near the base of our home. She exclaimed in horror, prompting us all to look in the direction of the snake. My youngest sister, too young to realize the danger to herself, ran close to the snake to grab her kitten away to safety. I have heard my mother retell that story and comment on how lucky we were that the cobra was a baby, because it did not strike either my sister or the kitten. Later that day, my father along with some Nigerian friends investigated the area only to discover a nest full of baby cobras, which they destroyed so the snakes would no longer be a threat to us as we came and went in and out of our house.

Another time, the older sister of a close friend suffered a cobra bite on her ankle while away at boarding school. The school personnel rushed her to the hospital in my town, a trip that took about an hour. The school nurse rode along, applying rotating tourniquets on the girl's leg just above the bite. She rotated, placing the tourniquet on and off, to restrict the poison from traveling up her leg while also allowing enough blood flow to keep the ankle and foot alive. God worked through the help of this nurse and the doctors at the hospital, and the girl recovered and did not even lose her leg. I remember visiting her at home and seeing her very swollen and discolored leg as she recovered from the bite.

Cobras were a very real and present danger to us. We were reminded to always be on the lookout for them. There were other types of poisonous snakes in the area, but in all my years in Africa, other than cobras I only remember seeing a green mamba in a tree once when it was pointed out to me.

When I came back to the States, I had a difficult time understanding why most people here are not afraid of snakes. My mother tried to explain that things were pretty opposite here. Whereas in Nigeria most snakes we might encounter were poisonous and only a few would be harmless, in the US most snakes were harmless with only a few being poisonous. Then, she told me a funny story of a harmless garter snake she had encountered as a child.

She came upon a garter snake that had swallowed an egg on one side of a fence, then slid under the fence and swallowed another egg on that side. She said the snake remained stuck with part of him on either side of the fence for hours, until the eggs finally digested. Her family laughed about that for years. She said her farmer father actually liked to find garter snakes in his garden because they kept the other critters away.

My grandfather may have liked snakes, but

they strike fear in my heart when I see them on a hot summer day lying on a rock or sidewalk warming themselves. I guess it's a response built into me from the earliest days of my life, and I will fear snakes the rest of my life.

The Bible tells us that there will come a time when no snake will be poisonous, and snakes will never harm anyone again. Isaiah 65:25 tells of a day when wolves and lambs will graze together; lions will eat straw like cows and snakes will no longer hurt or destroy any person or animal. What a wonderful time that will be. Until then, we must deal with snakes; real ones in the summertime, and the serpent of old—the enemy of our souls—who tries to harm and destroy us. May God help us discern the poisonous from the non-poisonous; the things that harm and should be avoided and the things that cannot be avoided which God has sent to challenge, teach, and grow us.

**Prayer:** Heavenly Father, nothing is beyond Your reach, and You are with us every minute of every day no matter what we may encounter in our lives. Walk with us and guide us in good days and bad. In

Jesus' name, amen.

**Thought for the Day:** Not every snake or frightening thing in life will harm us. Some will make us stronger, wiser, and more experienced.

## Day 3: Silk Spinners

by Shirley
Read Job 8:8-19

*What they trust in is fragile;*
*what they rely on is a spider's web.*
Job 8:14 (NIV)

You would think that since I was born in Nigeria and had encounters with a myriad of creatures of all shapes and sizes, that I would not be afraid of spiders. You would be very wrong. I am terrified of spiders. And yes, a granddaddy long-legs is just as terrifying as a black widow or brown recluse.

I often share with folks I have just met that I am terrified of spiders, and that if they toss rubber spiders at me, they may end up getting injured.

Interestingly, though, I am fascinated by and love to watch spiders weaving their webs—provided there is distance or thick glass between us.

When I lived in Alexandria, Virginia, my

house sat atop a hill. The dining room and living room were at the front of the house. There were two large bay windows across the front. If I was not coming home until after dark, or if I was expecting company to arrive after dark, I would leave the large spotlights on the outside corners of the house turned on.

I would turn the lights in the house off, leave the outside spotlights on, and watch spiders weaving their webs. I love watching spiders spin their webs. They are such graceful creatures. As they begin producing the webs, it looks like a choreographed dance. The web designs vary depending on the spider weaving it. The webs, of course, are woven so that the spider can entice unsuspecting prey to get stuck in the sticky web. Once caught in the web, the spider injects poisonous venom into its prey to paralyze and kill the insect so that the spider can consume it.

Would you believe I have a friend who is an arachnologist, a scientist who studies spiders and other arachnids? His goal when we first met was to get me to a point of not being terrified of spiders. He hoped that as he taught me all about spiders that

I would come to love them. Four decades later, he has not succeeded.

He did teach me to observe spiders and appreciate some things about spiders and their webs. As the spider spins his web, he puts a sticky fluid on the thread so that his prey gets stuck. The spider will leave one thread without sticky fluid on it, so he can get to the fly and not get stuck in his own web. After weaving his web, the spider crawls into a dark corner and hides, waiting for his prey. The spider has pulled one thread that leads to each section in the web and placed it under foot, so when that thread vibrates the spider knows where in the web to go.

An entry in my journal from decades ago says,

> A spider's web provides food, a place to nest, safety and security. A spider "takes hold" wherever the wind blows her. She has open access to palaces (Proverbs 30:28 KJV).

A handwritten note in my Bible beside Proverbs 30:28 says,

> God's word provides food for our souls and family, and gives us a strong, safe, and secure foundation for life.

Today's passage also speaks of a spider's web, but in a different way. Here, Job's friend Bildad the Shuhite is explaining to Job that he has obviously sinned and needs to repent. A handwritten note in my Bible beside Job 8:14 says, "If you do not have a strong spiritual foundation, you stand on weak ground." Although the spider can trust that he will be kept safe by holding on tightly to his web, Christ-followers cannot trust that we will be safe on such a frail and thin foundation.

My arachnologist friend also taught me that spiders can skillfully produce from within themselves beautiful webs woven of silk that are frail when the wind blows.

Just as the spider's job is to spin webs of silk, as Christ-followers we must be diligent to do what God has called us to do—glorify Him in and through all that we do and make disciple-makers.

Some spider's webs are beautiful and attract and entangle the spider's prey in order to feast on it. They are also frail, since they can be easily torn down or wiped away. Isaiah 59:5-6 tells us that we are sinful, and that all the work sinful man does to spin beautiful webs won't cover us like a garment nor give us shelter. The webs may snag and harm others, but they will not serve a godly purpose.

One morning as I was walking our dog Alex, I turned around to talk with him and coax him to come on. When I turned back around, I almost kissed a spider. I was staring straight into its eight eyes.

That's a good lesson for us to always be diligent and watching for the webs/snares of the evil one that wants to entrap us and entice us to sin.

**Prayer:** Heavenly Father, thank You for the spiritual lessons we learn from Your creation. Help us to rely upon You as our firm foundation to which we cling to withstand whatever comes into our lives. In Jesus' name, amen.

**Thought for the Day:** Hold fast to Jesus Christ, not

a frail spider's web.

# Day 4: The Wormwood and the Bitterness

by Harriet
Read Lamentations 3:19-24

*Remember my affliction and my wandering,*
*the wormwood and bitterness.*
*Surely my soul remembers and is bowed down within me.*
*This I recall to my mind, therefore I have hope.*
Lamentations 3:19-21 (NASB)

What a strange passage.

In these verses Jeremiah, the author of Lamentations, appears to recall times in his life that had been quite difficult for him, but then he makes an odd statement. He says that because of these memories, he has hope. Doesn't that seem strange to you? How can recalling difficult memories bring a person hope? It would seem to make more sense if these memories had brought despair to Jeremiah rather than hope. Yet hope is the very thing he claims to have because of the difficult times he had faced—what he calls the wandering, the wormwood and the bitterness.

When I first read this passage, it struck me as strange that hard, maybe even sad, memories could make someone hopeful. But then I, too, remembered some extremely difficult times in my life. One such time was nearly twenty years ago now. Someone I loved very much struggled greatly, and I struggled along with her. How I ached for my loved one and how I prayed. The situation seemed completely desperate at the time. And yet, somehow, God pulled her through. Today, I can look back and see God's hand in helping her. I know now what I didn't know then. I now know how God faithfully pulled her, and me, through those difficult days. I can rejoice at my loved one's healing and realize how blessed I am to have seen God's unfailing compassion.

I have faced other difficult days in my life, too. Some have been more challenging than others. Some of these were many years ago, others more recent, and still others continue even today. And, I know the years to come will not all be rosy and easy to handle. Yet, I can have hope because I now can remember specific problems I have faced in the past and see clearly how God worked in those situations.

With this perspective, it's easier to understand what Jeremiah meant when his recollection of troubled times in his life brought him hope. I, too, find hope for future difficult times that I may face bubbling up in my heart when I recall God's love and faithfulness in past situations.

How about you? Think back for a minute. Do you recall times of affliction; your times of wormwood and bitterness, as Jeremiah calls them? If so, then do you also have a testimony of God's faithfulness in those times? When we remember how God has helped us in the past, we see His compassions that are new every morning and indeed, we are filled with hope.

Not all memories are good memories. But, let's try to look at them through the lens of how God used those times in our lives to shape and mold us into the people we are today. He grew our faith and stamina through those times, and we can find hope for whatever we may face in our tomorrows.

**Prayer:** Great is Your faithfulness, O Lord. Thank You for all the difficulties You pull us through over and over again. Thank You for Your mercies that are new every morning. In Jesus' name, amen.

**Thought for the Day**: The same God who brought us through difficulties yesterday can be trusted with our tomorrows.

## Day 5: Paul and the Green Mamba

by Shirley

Read Numbers 21:4-9

*Just as Moses lifted up the snake in the wilderness,*
*so the Son of Man must be lifted up,*
*that everyone who believes may have eternal life in him.*
John 3:14-15

I have many vivid memories of our adventures as children growing up on the mission field in Nigeria. I remember standing on the ground under a tree with my brother Tim, watching our big brother Paul climb up and out onto a very high branch, just to see how far out he could climb without falling. He was boasting and laughing that he could climb higher and quicker than Beatrice, his pet baboon. He stopped and looked down at us and dared us to join him. Those dares normally were all the enticement we needed to overcome our fear of doing whatever crazy thing our big brother was doing.

He laughed, turned, and froze. We thought he

was mocking us for being afraid to climb up the tree. I moved closer to the trunk for a better view so I could figure out how I could climb up there with him. As I looked up all I saw was green leaves, but Tim yelled, "Stop! Look what's up there." Then I saw it. Paul was a few feet away from, and eye-to-eye with, a green mamba that was hanging from a limb above him.

At about the same time, Paul and Tim yelled "Maciji!" (The Hausa word for snake.) Dad, Mom, and various others came running from every direction. Dad was yelling for Paul to drop to the branch below him. Dad yelled, "Kids, step back, but don't take your eyes off the snake."

Paul scampered toward the trunk (he looked like a monkey or baboon) and down to a branch that was a safe jumping distance to the ground. I watched as that beautiful green mamba quickly and gracefully disappeared into the upper branches of the tree.

Now, if your snake anxiety has allowed you to get this far, you might be thinking, "What in the world does this story have to do with today's passage?" I'm glad you asked.

Snakes are fascinating creatures. While I am not afraid of snakes, I have a healthy respect for them because I understand how dangerous and deadly some snakes are. Any time the Nigeria missionaries and missionary kids get together now we hear familiar stories of snake encounters in Nigeria.

Although the bite of the West African green mamba delivers numerous cardiotoxins and neurotoxins that incapacitate the muscles of its prey, rendering it paralyzed or dead, it is beautiful. The richness of its green color highlights its graceful movements as it navigates through tree branches.

Dad's command, "Don't take your eyes off the snake" reminds me of the biblical account in today's passage. The Israelites were grumbling and complaining to God for leading them into the wilderness. God sent poisonous snakes that slithered into their camp and bit them.

Once the people realized they had sinned against God, they asked Moses to pray, asking the Lord to save them by taking all the snakes away from their camp. Moses interceded for the

Israelites, but God didn't answer the request in the way the people wanted. The snakes were not taken out of the camp.

Instead, God provided a way for them to be saved, but not from being bitten. Moses told the people to make a snake out of bronze and place it on a pole in the middle of the camp. Then, when the people were bitten by one of the poisonous snakes, they were to look up at the bronze snake and they would not die from the poisonous bite.

Just like the Israelites, before we became Christ-followers, we were poisoned by sin. There was nothing we could do to save ourselves but to look to the cross of Jesus where death was defeated. He arose and walked again on this earth, and He ascended to heaven where He now sits at the right hand of the throne of God interceding for us.

Why did Jesus die on the cross for us?

**Prayer:** Heavenly Father, thank You for pointing to salvation through Your Son, Jesus. Help us not to take our eyes off Jesus regardless of the situation in which we find ourselves. In Jesus' name, amen.

**Thought for the Day:** "For God so loved the world that he gave his only Son, that whoever believes in Him should not perish, but have eternal life. For God did not send His Son into the world to condemn the world, but in order that the world might be saved through Him" (John 3:16-17).

# Chapter 11

# Beneath the Summer Skies

## Day 1: Shadows

by Harriet
Read Psalm 23

*So do not fear, for I am with you; do not be dismayed, for I am your God. I will strengthen you and help you; I will help you with my righteous right hand.*
Isaiah 41:10

Summer days are longer, and so are the shadows that the summer sun casts.

Shadows can be fun, especially for children. I can remember walking with friends on sunny days during my childhood in Africa and playing a game where we tried to step on another person's shadow. We would yell out, "I got your arm," or "I stepped on your head," and the person whose shadow we had stepped on would fain injury. But most of the game we would sort of dance around trying to keep others from stepping on our shadows.

As a teenager, at some of the church youth social events, I used to play a game where each person had a balloon tied to one of their ankles. We would go around the room trying to step on, and pop, another person's balloon. The last person with an intact balloon still tied around his or her ankle won the game. I suppose my childhood shadow game was similar to this balloon game, but easier to play in a land where the sun shone brightly and constantly and where balloons were much harder to come by than sunshine.

But shadows can be scary, too. Just spend some time watching television movies. The bad guy is always lurking in the shadows. Shadows can obscure one's ability to see things clearly. Several years ago, I had a shadow encounter.

One sunny afternoon as I prepared dinner, I realized I was one ingredient short and needed to make a quick a run to the grocery store. I pulled out of my driveway, but then stopped abruptly. My car was equipped with one of those rear cameras which comes on automatically when I put the car in reverse. From that rear camera, there appeared to be a large, solid object in my driveway, which I was in danger of hitting. What in the world could it be?

I moved the gear shift to put my car in park and turned my head around to see with my own eyes what this large object might be. I found nothing but a shadow in the driveway. The late afternoon sun had caused the small tree near my driveway to cast a large shadow just where my car was pulling out. There was no solid object at all … just a shadow. I laughed out loud remembering how certain I had been that I was about to hit something with my car. I had nothing to fear after all. No large object had somehow been left in my driveway, and I was not going to hit anything as I backed out.

The twenty-third Psalm mentions shadows. It tells us that for believers, death is like a shadow. It is like the object I thought I saw in my driveway. It's just a shadow, with nothing really there to fear.

Today's key verse tells us why we do not need to be afraid of death, or shadows, or anything else. God is always with us. He will strengthen us, help us, and uphold us with His righteous right hand. There is nothing to fear in life or death.

**Prayer:** Thank You, Lord, for Your presence in our lives. Thank You for Your promises to always be with us. Calm our fears and bring to our minds Your comforting words. In Jesus's name, amen.

**Thought for the Day:** God is with us, no matter what we may be going through.

## Day 2: Hoisted Out of Danger

by Shirley
Read 1 John 5:1-5

*I know the LORD is always with me.*
*I will not be shaken, for he is right beside me.*
Psalm 16:8 (NLT)

One hot and humid summer afternoon, a friend and I decided to get our rafts and float down a portion of the Chattahoochee. We needed a break from our busy work schedules and church commitments, and we wanted a fun, laid-back day. We both drove our cars so we could leave one at the place where we would end our trip and drive the other one to our starting location.

We lathered up with sunscreen, donned our sunglasses, and got into the wonderfully cool water. We got on our rafts and began our leisurely float down the river. We chatted with each other and others who were floating down the river. When the sun and heat got to us, we just slid off our rafts and kicked around in the cool water. We were relaxed, just soaking in the river and the beautiful sky, and not paying attention to the signs indicating where we were in our journey.

Suddenly we were in the rapids. It was very rocky, and the water was swirling around all the rocks and making it difficult for us to stay on our rafts.

My friend said, "Uh, Shirley, we may have come further than we should have."

I was frightened. I tried to sit up with my legs dangling over the sides into the water, but my feet kept hitting rocks, so I had to bring them back up onto the raft. My friend's raft started losing air, so she and I were clinging to both rafts hoping we wouldn't drown.

Suddenly we heard voices yelling, "Hang on. We're coming to get you." There was a large raft heading toward us and the three young men in the raft were giving us instructions on what to do. They maneuvered beside my friend and pulled her into their raft. When she let go of my raft the swirling water began pulling me under. My knee found a jagged rock and decided to hit it very hard—twice.

I was almost in full panic mode when I heard a deep strong voice yell, “We’re right behind you. Reach back for my hand.” I was so frightened I couldn’t look back, and I was afraid that if I removed one hand from the raft I was holding onto for dear life, that I would surely drown.

I kept hearing that voice, “We’re right behind you. Reach back for my hand.” I finally reached my hand back, and the next thing I knew, the large raft hit up against my raft and two large hands grabbed me around the waist and hoisted me out of danger and into the safety of the large raft. The guys gave us water to drink and tended to the cuts on our feet, arms, and legs.

My friend and I learned some important lessons about rafting that day:

- Be sure you have the right equipment, and use it properly.
- Pay attention to your surroundings, signage, and what lies ahead.
- When help arrives, respond quickly to their instructions.

Sometimes in our spiritual lives, we get distracted or complacent so that we are not adequately prepared for the trials, struggles, and issues that come our way. We are caught off guard. We can quickly begin to feel as though we cannot bear the weight of whatever is going on, circumstances take over, fear overwhelms us, and we are rendered helpless.

Some of the same lessons my friend and I learned that day also apply to our spiritual lives, don't they?

We need to be sure we not only have the right equipment, but we need to use it properly. What's the right equipment for our spiritual lives? Prayer and God's word. It is not enough to just repeat rote words to God; we must learn to interact with God through prayer. Prayer involves us talking and listening to God. It also is not enough to simply have a Bible on a shelf or table at home or a Bible app on our phones. We must be engaged in consistent reading, studying, memorizing, contemplating, and meditating upon God's word—the Bible. As we consistently feed on God's word and pray, the Holy Spirit works to give understanding of God's word and the strength to apply it in whatever situation we find ourselves.

We also need to pay attention to our surroundings, but not to the point that we focus so intently on all the things going on around us that we begin to despair. Instead, we need to always be cognizant that the Lord is with us, and then we will not be shaken, because we know He is always with us (Psalm 16:8).

When help arrives, we need to respond quickly to the instructions of the helper. This is where our prayer and Bible reading, studying, memorizing, contemplating, and meditating come into play. Through His word, God has already told us what to do. The Holy Spirit will recall to our minds the things we have learned about God through His word, and He will enable us to exercise faith in God in every situation in which we find ourselves. I've heard it said that faith involves movement. Faith helps get us started and keeps us going in the strength of the Lord.

If you find yourself caught off guard and unable to bear the weight of what is going on as circumstances take over, fear overwhelms you, and you are rendered helpless, remember that God is right there with you and can help you walk through whatever you are facing, and sometimes, to hoist you out of danger.

**Prayer:** Heavenly Father, thank You for the way You use our everyday experiences to help us learn or to remind us of who You are and the biblical principles that are in Your word. Help us not to become complacent and contented to just flow through our lives without You. Teach us to depend upon You in all that we do. In Jesus' name, amen.

**Thought for the Day:** God is always with you to strengthen you to walk through the circumstances or to hoist you out of danger.

## Day 3: Unchanging

by Harriet
Read Micah 7:18-20

*Jesus Christ is the same yesterday and today,*
*yes, and forever.*
Hebrews 13:8 (NASB)

I used to love summer days when I was a child. I played outside all day under those clear, bright African skies, usually without shoes even though we were supposed to wear them to prevent parasites from gaining entry into our little bodies through the soles of our feet.

I had a lot of pets as a child that I played with all summer with reckless abandon. These included the usual, like a dog and cat, as well as guinea pigs, a tortoise, an African gray parrot, and a monkey. In the summertime, I spent much of my time dressing my pets, and adding things to their cages, or whatever environment they lived in. I can still remember working all summer one year fixing up the wooden box where my turtle lived. By the end of that summer, he had what seemed to my childish eyes, a luxury turtle apartment in which to live.

One of my favorite pet memories is of a chameleon I once had. It was more a temporary guest in my room than a pet, actually. In my tropical world chameleons could sometimes be found in the yard and caught by eager children, or they could be bought in the village night markets. The Nigerians used them for things other than pets. They may have been a delicacy to eat, but I suspect they may also have been used in some of the pagan rituals and spells. Whatever their intended purpose, some of the missionary kids bought them for pets.

I was never allowed to go to the night markets. My parents kept pretty strict bedtime hours. I came by my pet chameleon the honest way—I caught him. I can still remember how excited I was the day I caught the strange creature. I was walking along a road on my mission compound fondly referred to as Teak Boulevard because teak trees lined it on both sides. Suddenly, I spied the little guy standing perfectly still. He was brown in color in his effort to go unnoticed, but I saw him just the same.

Chameleons differ in appearance from lizards, though they are similar and can be mistaken for lizards unless a person gets a closer look at them. This one's brown appearance caught my attention because lizards are more often green. On closer inspection, I could see his funny feet that look like they are split into only two large fingers rather than several small ones like lizards have. His eyes, too, gave him away. They sit on either side of his face and can roll around and look in two different directions at the same time. I had become pretty skilled at catching lizards, so I tried my hand at catching the chameleon and met with success.

My mother allowed me to keep him for about a week before I had to set him loose once again. I had more fun that week watching him change colors. He could turn various shades of brown, green—including an almost neon green—blue, and yellow. I spent the week changing the little guy's environment to see him change colors. Once I even placed him on a purple piece of construction paper to see what he would do, but he just turned brown. That seemed to be his fallback color. I guess when in doubt, he decided to try and look like a stick.

Even as a child, I remember the lesson about God I learned from the chameleon. This strange creature can appear to be an assortment of different creatures and objects depending on what color he is. God is not like that. Though God created the chameleon and gave him his special ability, God never changes. God is God and never pretends to be anything else. Today's verse says this quite clearly, "Jesus is the same yesterday, today, and forever." Isn't that great news? Unlike a chameleon, God never changes, and according to Micah 7:18b, He takes delight in His unchanging love.

**Prayer:** Heavenly Father, thank You for remaining the same, no matter how my life or the world around me may change. Thank You for being the same God offering the same love to me when I call out to You. In Your Son's name, amen.

**Thought for the day:** Other things may change, but God never does.

## Day 4: Beside Still Waters

by Shirley
Read Psalm 23

*He makes me lie down in green pastures.*
*He leads me beside still waters.*
Psalm 23:2

The Twenty-Third Psalm is one of the most well-known passages in the Bible. It is read at funerals, at the side of death-beds, before surgeries, and during suffering and trials. I return to this Psalm time and time again for comfort, strength, and encouragement, and to remind me that the Good Shepherd—God—takes care of all my needs.

In today's passage David sings of the divine Good Shepherd who leads, guides, and sustains him. God guides David to green pastures of God's abundant provision and refuge with everything he needs. In God's pastures, we experience the presence of God and His care that meets our every need.

Matthew Henry tells us that "God makes his saints to lie down; he gives them quiet and contentment in their own minds, whatever their lot is; their souls dwell at ease in him, and that makes every pasture green."

Slowly flowing waters bring peace and relaxation to us; a sense of calmness. A handwritten note beside Psalm 23:2 in the margin of my Bible says "Hebrew—'beside waters of rest.'" The Good Shepherd, God, leads us to the still waters where we can rest because we know and trust Him and have confidence in Him. At these still waters, we can focus on Him without any distractions and rest from carrying our burdens that He will replace with His peace and rest (Matthew 11:28-30). God is the ultimate source of our peace and rest.

Summer is a great time to enjoy beautiful green pastures and the still waters of a lake, maybe getting cooled off by putting our feet into the water or having fun skipping stones across the surface.

For some time, I have had the honor of spending Fridays with a friend who has early-onset Alzheimer's and is still able to go on outings. After her hair appointment each week, we go to a local restaurant and do a Bible study together. I'm not sure what all from these studies she grasps, but I often see glimpses of understanding as she answers questions or makes comments.

One day, when her husband brought her to her hair appointment, he told me she was in a fog that morning. She didn't respond much as we traveled to the restaurant. We got our coffee and a snack, then settled down with our Bibles open to do our study.

All of a sudden, the restaurant filled with smoke and the fire alarm blared because a bagel had gotten stuck in the toaster. I could see the flaming bagel inside the toaster and knew that the employees would get it under control quickly, so I wasn't too concerned. But my friend got very agitated and kept saying "Help me. I'm scared."

I came around to her side of the table, took hold of her hand, turned to Psalm 23, and asked her to read it with me. Her voice was shaky at first, but got stronger as we read, "He leads me beside still waters." By the time we finished reading the Psalm, the chaos and smoke cleared from the restaurant, and for a few seconds in her mind as she said, "God loves me. I am not afraid." A little tear trickled down her cheek, and mine, too.

During times of desperate need, the word of God brings peace, rest, comfort, and encouragement for our souls. 2 Peter 1:3 tells us, "His divine power has granted to us all things that pertain to life and godliness, through the knowledge of Him who called us to His own glory and excellence."

I am so thankful for God's mercy, grace, and lovingkindness that give us the Holy Spirit-inspired Bible to break through the darkness and fog of Alzheimer's and all the other circumstances we face.

**Prayer:** Heavenly Father, thank You for giving us the Bible from which we not only learn about who You are, but are satisfied in You as we receive comfort, strength, and encouragement in our darkest moments. In Jesus' name, amen.

**Thought for the Day:** During our darkest moments, we can say, like my friend, "I am not afraid" because the Lord is the Good Shepherd who loves, cares, and provides for us.

## Day 5: Who's Afraid of the Dark?

by Harriet
Read Daniel 2:19-23

*Even the darkness is not dark to you;*
*and the night is as bright as day,*
*for darkness is like light to you.*
Psalm 139:12

"I'm scared, Daddy."

How many fathers have heard that over the centuries? Most of them, probably. When my sister was a child, she was afraid of the dark. Our home in Ogbomoso sometimes had unreliable electricity, especially during storms. Every time a storm came, our electricity flickered and invariably went out for long periods at a time.

Our mission had two compounds—the hospital and seminary compounds. My home was fortunate to be located on the hospital side, which had its own generator. The hospital, and the houses associated with it, usually regained electricity after a period of time once they got the generator at the hospital up and going. The seminary compound, on the other hand, sometimes lost electricity for much longer periods, since it got its electricity from the city. But even those of us able to benefit from the hospital generator occasionally lost electricity for up to an hour or two.

Those dark, stormy times filled my sister with fear. The world both outside and inside became dark. The flashing lightning and exploding thunder only made matters worse. My sister would crawl up in my father's lap and bury her face in his chest. One such time, in an effort to help ease her fears, my father told her that God was in the darkness, so she had nothing to be afraid of. Even when the world was dark, God was still there.

Another night, after the one described above, when things were calm and our electricity worked, my father found my sister pressing her face against the living room window looking out into the night. He peered out too, trying to see what she saw, but all he perceived was an ordinary night. Because of the lack of street lights or other outdoor lighting, the world outside the window was dark in spite of the twinkling stars in the skies. He asked her why she was looking outside. What was she trying to see? She replied, "I'm trying to see God." Then she added confidently, "God's out there in the dark, you know."

My sister had believed what our dad had told her—God is in the dark. So, in her childlike way, she tried her hardest to see Him.

Our passage today tells us that my father was right in telling my sister that God is in the dark, but it tells us even more about it. According to the passage, God is not only in the dark times of our lives, He also knows what's in the darkness because the darkness is not dark to Him.

Are you facing difficult circumstances and dark days right now? Are you straining to see God in the midst of your darkness? Keep looking toward God. The light dwells with Him. His wisdom can be found in His word. Pursue Him there and He will shine light on your situation.

**Prayer:** Almighty Father, You are the light of the world and the darkness has no hold on You. Help us to look to You today and any day that we find darkness trying to cast a shadow on our path. Thank You for Your eternal light. In Your Son's name, amen.

**Thought for the Day:** Jeremiah 29:13 tells us that when we seek God with all of our hearts, we will find Him. Let's press our faces against the window of His word and search for God with all our hearts.

Chapter 12

# School Days

## Day 1: School Days

by Harriet
Read Proverbs 20:11-15

*An intelligent heart acquires knowledge,*
*and the ear of the wise seeks knowledge.*
Proverbs 18:15

"School days, school days
Dear old Golden Rule days
Reading and 'riting and 'rithmetic
Taught to the tune of a hickory stick

You were my queen in calico
I was your bashful, barefoot beau
And you wrote on my slate, 'I love you Joe'
When we were a couple o' kids."

I grew up singing this little song. It was written in 1907 by Will Cobb and Gus Edwards and no, I am not that old. However, my parents knew the song, so I learned it from them. I used to sing "I love you, so" instead of "I love you, Joe," though. It always struck a chord in my heart, even as a child. The song depicts a mature couple who were apparently childhood sweethearts, thinking back on their childhood school days and the love they had shared. But the song speaks of more than just childhood love. It speaks of school days—reading, writing, and arithmetic. It speaks of the time in our lives when our main goal is to gain knowledge.

When I was a child, school started after Labor Day and marked the beginning of fall. Our school calendars have changed now. The new academic year begins in August for most, some places even in early August. As the summer is drawing to an end, and usually at its hottest, children find themselves back in school.

How well I remember my school years. In elementary school, I lived in Nigeria on a rather large mission compound with about a dozen other missionary families. Rather than having the parents homeschool their own children, we pooled our resources and had all the classes from first grade to fourth meet in the garage of one home. The woman whose family occupied that home had a teaching certificate and five children of her own, so she volunteered to teach all four classes in one spot. Essentially, I attended a one-room school house much like the American settlers did.

The mission had a boarding school where children in my area attended starting in the fifth grade, and then my family returned to America where I attended public school in my new hometown.

I loved my school days. I loved interacting with peers, and I also loved gaining knowledge. I have never outgrown these loves. I still enjoy interacting with people and gaining knowledge of any type, whether it's breakthroughs in science that I read about in the news, new insight into writing gained through studying the craft, or trying a new recipe. But, the best knowledge to gain is biblical knowledge. Through the years, I have participated in different Bible studies which, like school, all seem to follow the academic schedule.

The Bible speaks about knowledge in many places. One of the clearest points it makes about knowledge can be found in Proverbs 2:6, which tells us that knowledge comes from God. We do not need to follow the academic year in our pursuit of godly knowledge, but the start of the school year is always a good time to start a Bible study, too.

In your lifelong pursuit of knowledge, do not neglect pursuing biblical knowledge.

**Prayer:** Father, You have planted a desire for knowledge deep in the heart of people. Speak to us of our need to also grow in biblical knowledge and open up places and groups with whom we can study Your word. In Jesus' name, amen.

**Thought for the Day:** As school days begin again for so many, may we also begin a fresh study in God's word.

## Day 2: School? It's Still Summer!

by Shirley
Read Genesis 19:1, 12-28

*Fear not, for I am with you;*
*be not dismayed, for I am your God;*
*I will strengthen you, I will help you,*
*I will uphold you with my righteous right hand.*
Isaiah 41:10

Many years ago, as Mom and I were leaving the pharmacy, we saw a lady and her daughter whom we knew. It had been a while since we had seen them, so Mom asked if they wanted to go across the street and get something to drink and have a little visit.

We ordered our drinks and a couple of large french fries to share and started talking. Mom asked our friend if they had a good summer. She began to tell us about how she had not had time to enjoy summer at all. In June, her husband was offered a really good job with great benefits and a substantially larger salary. She went into detail about what his responsibilities would be in this new job.

"But?" Mom asked.

The lady said, "But, I don't want to move to another city. I love it here, my friends are here, and I love our house. My summer was ruined having to get things ready to move. I'm going but I'm not happy about it."

Our french fries came, and we shifted our attention to the ketchup and fries. The lady shifted the conversation off herself by asking Mom, "What are y'all doing today?"

Mom explained we were running several errands.

Mom asked when they were moving, and with tears in her eyes the lady said, "We pull out in the morning." Then looking at her daughter she said, "We start school the next day."

From the look on the girl's face you could tell she was trying to figure something out. Then all of the sudden she yelled, "School? It's still summer!" And the tears began to flow.

Using her finger to keep track she said, "December, January, February is winter. March,

April, May is spring. June, July, August is summer. September, October, November is fall. We go to school in fall, not summer."

Her mom tried to explain that although it was August, school started in two days. This time the girl's reaction was anger as she said, "Well, someone needs to tell them it is still summer, and you don't go to school in the summer."

We sat in silence for a few minutes and the little girl said, "Well, I know it's summer whether they do or not. My outside will be at school, but my inside will be in summer."

Mom realized that the little girl was probably anxious about the same things her mom was anxious about, so she began talking about the fun adventures our family had moving from place to place. The girl picked up the crayons and started coloring the children's menu that was on the table.

Mom shared with the other mom the difficulty of leaving family and the familiarity of the States to go to Nigeria. She talked about knowing the Lord was leading them to Nigeria and that He would help them do what He called them to do. She then told about how the Lord brought the Nigeria mission family around her to help her settle in and learn and get used to the culture. Then she said, "As we prepared to leave Nigeria and the precious mission family and Nigerian people, my heart was breaking. They had loved me so dearly, and I loved them dearly. But we knew the Lord was leading us to leave, and He would be with us wherever we went." Mom continued to explain how each change in our lives has its own difficulties—whether for something positive or something negative.

She said, "I don't want to be like Lot's wife (Genesis 19:26) and be attached to what's behind me, I want to move forward knowing God is with me."

Any time mom talked with this woman after their move and through the decades following it, the woman would remind mom of that conversation.

Mom was trying to let the woman know that it is hard to let go of familiar things whether it is changing jobs, homes, cities, or continents. Change is stressful for almost everyone. Even more difficult than leaving all those things behind is leaving—or putting off as the Bible says—sinful attitudes, behaviors, and habits.

Even though God sent the angels to warn Lot and his family of the coming judgment that would destroy Sodom and told them not to look back, Lot's wife did. We aren't told why she looked back, but maybe it was because she had strong emotional ties to all the people, things, and experiences she was leaving behind.

When you face a change or that sinful habit is tugging at your heart, walk confidently into your future knowing, "The Lord is my rock and my fortress and my deliverer, my God; my rock in whom I take refuge, my shield, and the horn of my salvation, my stronghold" (Psalm 18:2). When God calls you to change or move, He will guide you and give you the mercy, grace, peace, strength, and stamina to do whatever He is asking you to do.

**Prayer:** Heavenly Father, change is difficult for us, we would rather hold onto the familiar and stay where we are. Give us the faith to step out and follow You. Your guidance, strength, and stamina will enable us to move where You are leading us and to change as Your Holy Spirit convicts us of our sin. In Jesus' name, amen.

**Thought for the Day:** "… walk in all the way that the Lord your God has commanded you, that you may live, and that it may go well with you, and that you may live long in the land that you shall possess" (Deuteronomy 5:33).

## Day 3: America's Favorite Pastime

by Harriet
Read Colossians 3:14-17

*Whatever your hand finds to do,*
*do it with all your might....*
Ecclesiastes 9:10a

The clicking of cleats as they walk across a concrete path to the football field, the clash of helmets, a cheering crowd, the smell of hot dogs and popcorn—how I love the sights, sounds, and smells of football games. I'm not the biggest sports enthusiast in the world, but I do like football, especially high school football.

My family came back to the States when I was in middle school, which we called junior high back then. Football was huge in my new hometown. Every boy wanted to play football, and every girl wanted to be a cheerleader. The high school had a tradition of not only winning year after year, but also accumulating many state championships under the leadership of a much-loved, somewhat legendary coach who had moved on a couple of years before I got there.

I worked so hard trying to make the cheerleading squad, and I finally made it my last year of middle school and again my junior and senior years of high school. My senior year, our team once again claimed the AAA state title with a Cinderella team in a come-from-behind final game. It is still one of the highlights of my life.

As an adult, I work as a substitute teacher for a Christian school. I substitute in both middle school and high school. Our football team, too, has been blessed with success, winning two AA state championships in recent years. So, attending high school football games and cheering on the home team is still something I am blessed to do every fall, though I cheer from my seat on the bleachers now instead of from the field.

Football is fondly referred to as "America's favorite pastime" by many, though the term was actually first used for baseball in the 1850s. Today, it is hotly debated as to which sport can make the claim. Baseball has been American's pastime longer, but football garners more viewers and lays claim to more revenue from all sources, including merchandise and ticket sales. Wherever the truth may lie, fall is when football shines.

Does God care about football, or any of our pastimes or hobbies? Though I would not go far enough to agree with people who might argue that God is for or against certain teams, I think He cares about His people and made us creatures who enjoy hobbies. Our passage today sheds light on how we should act in small things in our lives; how we should live our lives whether we are at church worshiping Him or in the bleachers watching our favorite team play. Colossians 3:14 tells us to put on love, and verse 15 says to let Christ's peace rule in our hearts . . . whether our team is winning or losing. And, verse 17 says that whatever we do, we should do it in the name of Jesus. What an awesome responsibility to realize that we bear Christ's name as Christians, and we represent Him in everything we do, even if it's just cheering on our team. Furthermore, others are watching how we behave, even—and maybe especially—when we are losing.

**Prayer:** Father, as school starts, we are faced with many new seasons—autumn coming soon, new academic year, and new sports seasons. Help us to remember that we represent You. Help us to behave in a gracious and respectful manner whether things are going the way we would like or not. In Jesus' name, amen.

**Thought for the Day:** You represent Christ to a fallen world, and they are watching.

## Day 4: As Unto the Lord

by Shirley
Read Colossians 3:1-17

*And whatever you do, in word or deed,*
*do everything in the name of the Lord Jesus,*
*giving thanks to God the Father through him.*
Colossians 3:17

I was sitting in the waiting room at the dentist office about a week before school started. I had broken off a piece of a tooth, so they were working me in, which meant I sat in the waiting room for a good while.

When I sat down, there was a lady sitting nearby with her laptop open. Her nails clicked the keyboard as she typed furiously, and from time-to-time she would release a heavy sigh.

A second lady came in and sat down across from the first. She pulled out her laptop said to the first lady, "I'm a teacher, and the children will be there next week. I have so much to get done."

The first lady said, "I'm a teacher, too," (and

she told her where she taught) "and I was just emailing some of the parents whose children will be in my class. I am so excited that many of them are Christ-followers. I am so thankful I'm a teacher. It's going to be a great year."

"I hate teaching, and I don't like children," was the second teacher's response. Then she proceeded to talk about how awful her school was and how the "big wigs" think they know it all, and the parents are stupid, and the students should all be in jail. "I go to church, too, but these folks are hopeless causes."

As she spoke, her words and tone became more and more venomous, and it felt like she was sucking all the air out of the room.

Thankfully, they called me back, and I didn't have to hear any more. As I left, I winked at the Christ-following first lady and mouthed, "I'm praying."

After they fixed my tooth, I saw the Christ-follower sitting in the hygienist chair. I stuck my head in the door and told her how thankful I am that we have Christ-followers who are willing to invest in the lives of our children and their parents.

Now, before I go any further, I want you to know I understand that everyone can have a bad day, and I realize that teaching is a very difficult profession. Teachers have to deal with so many things such as: state and federal mandates, lack of supplies, sometimes poor facilities, children who are so hungry they can't think, children who are disrespectful, parents who cause problems, and so on.

The juxtaposition of these teacher's attitudes about the beginning of school was astounding. I have thought about that exchange off-and-on for a good while. I've wondered why each teacher wanted to teach in the first place. I've wondered if the unhappy teacher ever loved teaching. I've wondered how the children and parents in both teacher's classes fared during that school year.

I am blessed in so many ways, including that I love my job as a financial secretary, and the other things I do: church pianist, Sunday school and Bible study teacher, biblical counselor, conference teacher/speaker, and writer. I have also been in jobs that I detested and worked with people whom I didn't like very well.

Let's see what God calls Christ-followers to all the time, whether they love what they are doing or detest it. The bottom line is that we are here on earth to glorify God in and through all that we do. In biblical counseling sessions, I sometimes ask "For what are you doing all of this?" I'm hoping to get a glimpse into their motivation for doing what they are doing.

The responses to that question are as varied as the number of responders. Sometimes, someone does something to get recognition from her boss or spouse, or sometimes it is to impress someone. These reasons are all worldly reasons and will eventually crumble.

The Apostle Paul says that honoring our Savior and Lord, Jesus, is to be our motivation. That means that everything we think, say, and do is done in Jesus' name. Because God prepares, equips, and leads us, we can walk into whatever situation He has placed us with confidence that He will help us. We must depend upon God and not our own knowledge, understanding, ability, or skill. He often calls us to work outside of our comfort zone. Our gratitude to Him for all He has done to provide for us fuels our passion to serve Him more.

What is your motivation for doing the things you do?

**Prayer:** Heavenly Father, thank You for preparing, equipping, and leading us throughout our lives. Give us grateful hearts as we do the things You call us to do. Teach us to do everything for Your glory and honor. In Jesus' name, amen.

**Thought for the Day:** "Whatever you do, work heartily, as for the Lord and not for men, knowing that from the Lord you will receive the inheritance as your reward. You are serving the Lord Christ" (Colossians 3:23-24).

## Day 5: Safe in God's Hands

by Harriet
Read Psalm 91:1-4, 14-16

*For he will command his angels concerning you*
*to guard you in all your ways;*
*they will lift you up in their hands, so that you*
*will not strike your foot against a stone.*
Psalm 91:11-12 (NIV)

I stretched out alongside a pool to enjoy a last vacation of the summer. Next week, my children would be starting back to school and we wanted one more little escape to the beach before we had to face school and all the responsibilities it brings.

Splash! My eight-year-old hit the water and swam to the edge to do another back flip. With natural athletic ability, he had been doing back flips at the deep end of the pool all day. I sat at the shallow end keeping an eye on my preschool daughter, and was enjoying seeing the fun my son was having at the other end of the pool. I watched him climb out of the pool, dart a few feet away and start his run toward the pool to do another back flip, but this time, something went wrong. I knew it the minute he jumped into the air to flip. He started his flip too far from the edge of the pool. I watched in horror as he hit the back of his head on the side of the pool when he came down. I saw his head jerk forward as he sank into the pool.

My brother-in-law, Teddy, saw it too, and ran toward the pool from his seat much closer to the deep end. Teddy reached out as my son floated up in a sitting position with his right arm extended upward holding his hand in a tight fist. Teddy grabbed my son's extended arm and pulled him out of the water.

My husband and I rushed our son to the emergency room, where they took x-rays of his skull and cleaned and stitched his head wound. His skull had not been broken, and we were sent home to recuperate. That's how it happened. I remember it clearly.

However, my son told me a different story a few days later. He said he felt his head hit the side of the pool and remembered sinking to the bottom. Then, he opened his eyes under water and looked up. He said he saw a hand reaching down to him, so he grabbed the hand and felt his body being pulled upward. He thought it had been his uncle's hand. "Uncle Teddy reached way down into the pool, and I grabbed his hand," my son told me, obviously believing everything he said.

But I know differently. The hand that brought my son up was not his uncle's. His uncle could have never reached all the way down to the deep end of the pool, and I saw it happen. I saw my son's fisted arm float up out of the water and watched Teddy grab it and pull him to safety.

Who reached down into the deep end of that pool? Whose hand did my son grab? Personally, I think it was an angel, sent from God to save my son from drowning.

The emergency room personnel asked my son what color stitches he wanted. He chose bright yellow. My son started school that year with bright yellow stitches in a shaved place in the back of his head. He thought it was cool and he became an instant celebrity among his third-grade friends. And, every time I saw those stitches, I thanked God for saving my son. As a grown man, he now chooses to shave his head, and that one-inch scar is visible and still reminds me of how God sent an angel to help him in his time of need. I am so thankful for a loving God whose angels lift us up in their arms, sometimes literally.

**Prayer:** Thank You Lord, for Your protection in our time of need. We love You. In Jesus' name, amen.

**Thought for the Day:** God is still in the business of performing miracles.

## Chapter 13

# *Autumn's Here*

## Day 1: Goodbye . . . Hello

by Shirley
Read Philippians 3:12-21

*But our citizenship is in heaven,*
*and from it we await a Savior, the Lord Jesus Christ.*
Philippians 3:20

Mom and Dad kept talking about us "going home," which meant going back to the States—their home, but it wasn't really mine. Although it happened many decades ago when I was very young, certain things about my family packing up and leaving Nigeria to come home to the States for good are indelibly burned into my memory. The flurry of activity as we packed things for transport to the States, the discussions about what furniture or household item this missionary family or that one could use, what pieces of our clothing we would leave behind for other missionaries or missionary kids and who would get our toys since we would leave most of them behind.

As word spread throughout the area, a constant stream of people came by to see us. Over and over my parents, the missionaries, and the precious Nigerian people would give thanks to God for the time they had together in Nigeria and for the many things the Lord had done for them and taught them. I have memories of us standing on the front porch and watching as a dear one walked away and disappeared from sight.

Although space does not allow me to share many other memories here, I think you can understand the myriad of emotions that flooded all of our hearts as we said our goodbyes in Nigeria and headed to the States.

As I grew older, I realized I had not really understood what was happening back then. You see, in my mind, we were leaving our familiar home to go to a strange place filled with many unknowns, while we were in fact leaving our temporary home in Nigeria to go to our more permanent home in America.

That's the truth we see in today's Scripture passage. This earth is only our temporary home, heaven is our permanent, eternal home. In John

13:33, Jesus tells His disciples that He is going away and that they can't go with Him. Then, Simon Peter asked where Jesus was going and why he couldn't follow Him (verses 36-37).

Apparently, the news that Jesus was leaving them frightened the disciples, because Jesus tells them, "Let not your hearts be troubled. Believe in God, believe also in me" (John 14:1). Jesus continues to explain, "In my Father's house are many rooms. If it were not so, would I have told you that I go to prepare a place for you? And if I go to prepare a place for you, I will come again and will take you to myself, that where I am you may also be" (John 14:2-3).

What an amazing and comforting truth. Our Savior, Jesus Christ, preparing our home in heaven for our arrival. From other places in Scripture we know that while Jesus Christ is preparing a place for us, the Holy Spirit is at work in our hearts to prepare us for our home in heaven by bringing us to Christ and making us into His image.

In Acts 20:32, Paul speaks to the Ephesian elders and commends them ". . . to God and to the word of his grace, which is able to build you up and to give you the inheritance among all those who are satisfied." Our salvation not only brings redemption, it also builds us up in our faith through the process of sanctification—being made into God's image. Then Jesus Christ will return, and we will be at home for eternity in heaven with Him.

What does this mean for us as we live here in our temporary home on earth? It means that we are to live our lives with eternity, our eternal home, in view.

I have read that Jonathan Edwards often prayed, "O God, stamp eternity on my eyeballs," to remind himself to view everything and everyone with eternal significance This quote is handwritten in my Bible beside 2 Corinthians 4:18: "For this light momentary affliction is preparing for us an eternal weight of glory beyond all comparison, as we look not to the things that are seen but to the things that are unseen. For the things that are seen are transient, but the things that are seen are eternal."

Some of us are sad to say goodbye to summer and hello to autumn just as I was reluctant to say goodbye to my home in Nigeria and hello to my home in America. There are also times that I am reluctant to think about saying goodbye to my home here on earth, until I remember how glorious it will be when God calls me to my heavenly home.

**Prayer:** Heavenly Father, it is often difficult for us to say goodbye when we have felt safe, comfortable, and at home. Help us learn to say our goodbyes here on earth and remember that the things of this earth are only temporary. Thank You for preparing us a place in heaven and for our salvation and sanctification that prepare us to come live in our heavenly home. In Jesus' name, amen.

**Thought for the Day:** Jesus has prepared your heavenly home and you, so that you can spend eternity in heaven with Him.

## Day 2: Clear Autumn Skies

by Harriet
Read 1 Corinthians 13:9-12

*For now we see in a mirror dimly, but then face to face. Now I know in part; then I shall know fully even as I am fully known.*
1 Corinthians 13:12

I don't pay that much attention to the weather. Oh, I know it's hot in the summer and cools down in the fall, but before I was married, if you had asked me which season is more likely to have overcast skies and which is more likely to have clear skies, I would not have known how to answer. But John, the man I married, was learning to fly when we started dating. I remember the day he made his first solo fight. Flight instructors tear off a piece of your shirt when you solo for the first time, at least they did back then. I can still see him with his shirt torn and a huge smile on his face.

Autumn is the answer to the question posed in the paragraph above about which season has the most days with clear skies. When my new husband first got his pilot license, he did not have his instrument rating, which meant he could only fly if the weather was nice and he could actually see the world around him so as to know where to land. He used to have me looking out the window searching on the ground trying to find the airport strip below us. He loved those clear autumn days when he could fly with only his visual rating.

Later, John got his instrument certification and then was able to fly using the instruments to guide him. That was a whole new experience for me. I suppose we all fly like that when we fly in large airplanes, but there was something unnerving about sitting in the front seat of a plane, next to the pilot, keenly aware that we could not see more than two feet in front of us because of dense clouds. I had to learn that the instruments my husband used to fly by were reliable and could be trusted. I was always more comfortable sitting in my husband's airplanes on clear days when I could look out my window and see things plainly.

Today's passage in 1 Corinthians talks about seeing dimly and only knowing in part. Our lives are filled with times when we cannot see things clearly. We sometimes do not know which decision to make, which option to choose, or how something is going to turn out. Like pilots who fly with the help of instruments, we must learn to trust the guidelines God has laid out for us in His word. We are living by faith, not by sight, as 2 Corinthians 5:7 says.

Life might seem easier if we only knew how things were going to turn out once we made one decision or another. But God doesn't always give us clear days. Yet, on the unclear ones, He lays out guidelines in His word and gently guides us on our way, as Isaiah tells us when He says, "And your ears shall hear a word behind you, saying, 'This is the way, walk in it,' when you turn to the right or to the left." Maybe, instead of wishing for clear days in our lives, we should work at learning to fly using the instruments God gave us to help guide us during those overcast and stormy days. Maybe we should work on hearing God's still, small voice when He whispers to us as to how we should go forward in a given situation.

**Prayer:** Almighty God, You know all that we do not know. You hold our lives and our futures in Your hands. We don't see the future and sometimes we don't even have clarity about what we are experiencing in the moment in which we are living. But, You have given us Your word and the ability to commune with You in prayer, which are instruments we can use to help guide us when things seem unclear. Thank You. In Jesus' namc, amen.

**Thought for the Day:** How well do you navigate in stormy times? Do you have your spiritual instrument certification yet?

## Day 3: Stepping Into a New Season

by Shirley
Read Matthew 14:22-33

*Commit your way to the LORD;*
*trust in him, and he will act.*
Psalm 37:5

Many years ago, I was working in Old Town Alexandria, Virginia, and decided it was time to move a little closer to my family who lived in Alabama. I had accumulated a large number of frequent flyer points, so I decided to use those to fly to Atlanta, Georgia, and see what job options were open for me there. Because I had worked in several organizations through the years, both secular and religious, that provided invaluable experience and opportunities to hone and enhance my skills and enrich my work experience, I was able to line up sixteen interviews over a four-day period. I was off to Atlanta.

I was so grateful that I received several job

offers and accepted the one I wanted and signed a lease on an apartment before I left Atlanta. The next few weeks were a bit of a whirlwind as I resigned from my job, began packing and making arrangements to move to Atlanta.

Two and a half weeks later, the loaded moving truck pulled out and I headed for Atlanta. After several days of settling in and unpacking, I got up Monday morning, excited about this new season in my life.

I stopped a couple of blocks away from my new office to get some coffee before work. I struck up a conversation with a lady and told her I had just moved to town for a new job. She began talking about how she could never leave what she knew and go somewhere else. In a few minutes, I left and drove to my new office.

I walked across the parking lot to the office building. As I got about five feet away from the entrance, I started thinking about leaving my comfortable life, how quickly this move had happened, and all the unknowns about the job and city. I got very scared, my heart began racing, and I was struggling to catch my breath. I felt flushed, and I was nauseated. I guess I looked pretty bad because a lady came up and asked if I was feeling okay and offered to call 911 if I needed help.

She walked over to a bench just outside the building entrance and sat down with me. I explained I had just moved to town and was starting a new job and that I was suddenly in a panic about it all. She said, "Let me pray for you." She prayed a beautiful praying asking God to calm my nerves and help me as I started my new job.

We chatted a few more minutes as I told her I needed to dwell on the facts. The Lord led me to move and provided the job and an apartment. She walked into the building with me, introduced me to the receptionist, and walked to the Human Resources office with me. I had a great first day. The Lord sent me many new friends and a good church home. I loved my time in Atlanta.

It is likely that we have all experienced times where it seemed as though we stepped off firm group onto very shaky ground. I knew the Lord's hand was involved in all the things that happened and culminated in my being in Atlanta. But, at the moment I was to literally step into my new season of life, it seemed as though I had waded into the deep middle of a swiftly moving river. I panicked and tried to not be swept away by the current.

In today's Scripture reading, we read the account of the disciples being out at sea in their boat and being "beaten by the waves." They were very frightened when they saw what they thought was a ghost walking on the water. Jesus told them, "Take heart; it is I. Do not be afraid."

Peter said, "Lord, if it is you, command me to come to you on the water." And Jesus said, "Come." Peter got out of the boat and was walking on water toward Jesus. Then, he began noticing the strong wind stirring up waves in the water. He was afraid, and as he started sinking he yelled out for the Jesus to save him from drowning.

As Jesus took ahold of Peter's hand he said, "O you of little faith, why did you doubt?" They got into the boat, and the wind stopped blowing so violently.

Although we're not told exactly what Peter was thinking when he began to sink, I imagine he experienced some of the same thoughts and emotions I had that morning as I approached the entrance to my new job.

A handwritten note beside Matthew 14:32 in my Bible says, "As a fisherman, the boat was a comfortable and safe place for Peter. He didn't have to have faith to stay in the boat. Even when a storm was raging and the boat was being tossed around, in his own strength he could do what was necessary to save himself from harm."

The moment he stepped out of the boat and onto the water he was in an unfamiliar situation he had never before experienced.

We know Peter had faith in Jesus because he told Jesus He could prove it was really Him by commanding Peter to come to Him. So, we can read into Peter's statement that He knew Jesus was able to get him from the boat to Himself—he had faith in Jesus.

Peter's faith in the Lord waivered, and he didn't give totally of himself to follow Jesus' command. No matter the circumstance in which we find ourselves or how shaky—or watery—the ground on which we step is, if the Lord led us there, we can trust His leading and confidently follow Him wherever He leads us. Stepping out in faith, even when the ground seems rocky, actually lands us on solid ground as we trust in our Rock, Jesus Christ. This holds true when we are entering into a situation that is uncertain or looks dangerous, for God can lead us to the safety and rest of solid ground.

How do we keep our faith strong? By being consistent in praying and reading, studying, memorizing, contemplating, and meditating upon God's word, we bear fruit in many areas of our lives and our faith in God grows stronger.

**Prayer:** Heavenly Father, thank You that when You call us onto shaky ground, we can trust You to bring us to safety. May our faith in You grow stronger so that when You call and lead us into something that we are quick to move out in obedience, trusting Your enablement and provision. In Jesus' name, amen.

**Thought for the Day:** "My soul continually remembers it and is bowed down within me. But this I call to mind, and therefore I have hope" (Lamentations 3:20-21).

## Day 4: As the Days Grow Shorter

by Harriet
Read John 9:1-5

*We must work the works of him who sent me while it is day; night is coming when no one can work.*
John 9:4

Fall is fast approaching, and with it come shorter days. The sun sets a little earlier each day. Then as we are on the verge of winter, in many places we turn our clocks back and suddenly it grows dark so early it almost feels like darkness falls in the middle of the afternoon.

Personally, I like sunshine. Ecclesiastes 11:7 says, "Light is sweet, and it is pleasant for the eyes to see the sun." This could be my life's verse, because I love the sunshine and daylight. I'm joking about it being my life's verse, but it does resonate with my heart, and personally I relish those long summer days and dread the coming of shorter days.

But, there is more than just personal taste about sunshine in the message of today's key passage. In these verses in John 9, Jesus encourages His disciples to work while there is time. Have you ever heard the expression, "Make hay while the sun shines?" It's an old saying that means to take advantage of the chance to do something when you have the opportunity, or the chance may pass you and you may not have that opportunity to do that particular thing again. This is part of the message Jesus is giving to His disciples, but He specifically mentions doing the works of "him who sent me" while there is an opportunity to do them. This is, of course, a reference to God as the one who sent Jesus to the earth. So, Jesus is telling us to do God's work while the opportunity is before us.

My parents, Shirley's parents, and many other committed Christ-followers set out for Nigeria and other countries to share the gospel with people who had never heard of Jesus. In the case of our Nigerian mission, my parents and others first went there some time in the 1950s. But in 1967, the Biafran War broke out. In the years that followed, many doors for outreach closed, missionaries were evacuated from various places, and others who had gone home on furlough were not given visas back into the country. The days of their opportunity to share the gospel and to disciple new believers had grown short. They were quickly running out of daylight. Suddenly, they became keenly aware that the days they had spent doing the works God had sent them to do were numbered.

During the peaceful days before the war, the missionaries had no idea that what seemed like endless days ahead of them to reach the lost were not endless at all. How many times did one of them decide to put off for tomorrow some work they were doing because they were tired or busy, and they were certain they could finish it later only to one day realize they had run out of tomorrows? Suddenly, the work they had done while they had the chance mattered greatly. When they could no longer teach, preach, and disciple would those who had already been reached carry on their ministries?

We may not be missionaries, but all of life is like that. I once had babies and small children living in my home whose little hearts, minds, and personalities I could mold, teach, and shape. Those days seemed long and endless. Yet today, all of my children are grown and some even have children of their own. Where did those days go? How did they speed by me so fast? I can no longer mold or shape my children; the most I can do now is love them and pray for them as they make their own adult decisions.

God has work to be done by us. May we learn to seize each and every opportunity.

**Prayer:** Heavenly Father, open our eyes to the doors You have opened for us and the opportunities You have laid before us—the works You have for us to do. Then, open our hearts to want to work while the opportunity still exists. In Jesus' name, amen.

**Thought for the Day:** Seize the day before it's gone.

## Day 5: Savoring Autumn

by Shirley
Read Psalm 34

*Oh, taste and see that the LORD is good!*
*Blessed is the man who takes refuge in him!*
Psalm 34:8

Just as the crispness of autumn was settling over Alabama, some friends who lived down in Naples, Florida, came to visit for four days. This couple was anxious to experience autumn in Alabama. So, Mom and Dad helped make a list of things that would help them experience autumn. In the next few days, they picked apples, went to a pumpkin patch, made apple butter and apple sauce, and they went to Noccalula Falls and Little River Canyon and took a lot of pictures of the beautifully colored leaves on the trees. They were worn out when they loaded their car to head back home. They had rushed through autumn in Alabama.

A few weeks later, Mom received a letter from them expressing how much they enjoyed their trip, but they said, "We fast-forwarded through autumn in Alabama." Next year we need to come for a couple of weeks and savor autumn in Alabama."

While we may not be fast-forwarding through autumn the way our Florida friends did, we often get so busy with school, church, and community activities that we rush from one thing to the next without really savoring each one. And before we know it, autumn is over.

I enjoy seeing the pumpkins, Indian corn, autumn flowers, and the leaves turn from green to the beautiful colors of yellow, gold, red, purple, and orange. The crispness of the air is exhilarating. I love soaking in the beauty and smells of autumn.

We sometimes get so busy with family, church, school, and community activities that we don't take time to savor God. How do we savor God?

Today's passage is David's song of thanksgiving that God rescued him. God has promised to rescue, protect, supply, and sustain those who trust in Him. Our key passage invites us to savor God as we, "taste and see that the Lord is good!" David is saying, "Come experience the amazing goodness of God." We are to trust in God, get to know Him personally through the Holy Spirit-inspired Bible and prayer, believe and obey His word, and experience His goodness firsthand.

While we are struggling, wounded, and suffering in the midst of trials, or so busy we can barely think, we may not be able to taste or see the goodness of God. Yet, we know He and His goodness are ever-present. Romans 8:28 reminds us that, "for those who love God all things work together for good, for those who are called according to his purpose."

It is important to note here that things working together for our "good" doesn't mean that we necessarily think it's good. Instead, it carries the connotation of those things working together for our sanctification, to strengthen our spiritual lives. This knowledge encourages us to trust Him with everything and to thank Him for everything.

As we accept the invitation to "taste and see the Lord" and get to know Him personally, in grateful response, we will give glory and honor to Him and share this invitation with others.

Are you familiar with the account in Matthew 16 of Jesus telling the disciples about His death and resurrection? Peter pulled Jesus aside and rebuked Him, saying that it wouldn't happen to Him. Then in verse 23 Jesus says to Peter, "Get thee behind me, Satan: thou art an offence unto me: for thou savourest not the things that be of God, but those that be of men" (KJV).

Jesus is saying your mind is on things of the world or men instead of on Him. Psalm 1:2 tell us that blessed is the man who delights in God's word and meditates on it day and night. God's word is always foremost in his mind, therefore, "He is like a tree planted by streams of water that yields its fruit in its season, and its leaf does not wither. In all that he does, he prospers" (Psalm 1:3).

In my mind, another passage puts all this together, "But thanks be to God, who in Christ always leads us in triumphal procession, and through us spreads the fragrance of the knowledge of him everywhere. For we are the aroma of Christ to God among those who are being saved and among those who are perishing" (2 Corinthians 2:14-15). As Christ-followers we taste and see God as we spend time in His word and in prayer, then we go out into the world and spread His sweet fragrance everywhere.

**Prayer:** Heavenly Father, thank You for allowing us to know You personally. Give us a passion to savor You so that we can spread the sweet fragrance of You wherever we go. In Jesus' name, amen.

**Thought for the Day:** As you go through your day, savor the beauty of autumn and remember to savor God.

# Hymns and Songs

"As Pants the Hart for Cooling Stream," Nathan Tate and Nicholas Brady

"Deep and Wide," Sidney E. Cox

"I've Got the Joy, Joy, Joy, Joy, Down in My Heart," George W. Cooke

"Jesus Loves Me," Anna Bartlett Warner

"Jesus Loves the Little Children," C. H. Woolston

"Jesus Shall Reign," Isaac Watts

"Peace," Barney E. Warren

"Revive Us Again," William P. Mackay

"School Days," Will Cobb and Gus Edwards

"Soldiers of Christ Arise," Charles Wesley

"There is Sunlight on the Hilltop," Mrs. M. T. Haughey

"This Little Light of Mine," Harry Dixon Loes

# Acknowledgments

The Lord has been gracious to plant seeds of friendship in our hearts when we were young children and to deepen those bonds through our relationship with Him and each other. We are grateful for the opportunity to collaborate on another devotional.

We are thankful for Harriet's daughter, Kristin Michael, for creating the beautiful illustrations you will find throughout the devotional.

We are grateful for the support, encouragement, and guidance our Nigeria missionary-kid cousin, Baker Hill, provided during the process of writing this devotional.

We appreciate the contribution of our editor, Julie Hausmann, who helped us refine our manuscript.

We are indebted to our friend and publisher, Marji Laine Clubine, for her encouragement and direction as she worked tirelessly helping us to bring this devotional to print and for the beautiful cover design.

# About the Authors

## Shirley Crowder

Shirley Crowder was born in a mission guest house under the shade of a mango tree in Nigeria, West Africa, where her parents served as missionaries. She and co-author Harriet E. Michael grew up together on the mission field and have been life-long friends. Shirley is passionate about disciple-making, which is manifested in and through a myriad of ministry opportunities: biblical counseling, teaching Bible studies, writing, and music.

She is a biblical counselor and commissioned by and serves on the national Advisory Team for The Addiction Connection. She is an award-winning writer who has had several of her articles appear in "Paper Pulpit" in the Faith section of *The Gadsden Times*, and in a David C. Cook publication. She also writes articles for Life Bible Study, InspiredPrompt.com, Woman's Missionary Union, and TheAddictionConnection.org. She has authored, co-authored, or contributed to seven books.

Shirley has spiritual children, grandchildren, and even great-grandchildren serving the Lord in various ministry and secular positions throughout the world.

**Follow her on:**

**Facebook:** /shirleycrowder

**Twitter:** @ShirleyJCrowder

**Blog:** www.throughthelensofScripture.com

**Amazon:** /author/shirleycrowder

# Harriet E. Michael

Harriet E. Michael was born in Joinkrama, Nigeria, deep in the African jungle in the Niger River delta, where her father served as the only missionary doctor at that station. A few years later, the mission moved the family to a larger hospital in Ogbomoso. Co-author Shirley Crowder and her family lived right across the dirt road. The two children became constant playmates. Today they continue to enjoy their lifelong friendship.

Harriet is a multi-published, award-winning writer and speaker. She has authored or co-authored seven books (six nonfiction and one novel) with several more under contract for future release. She is also a prolific freelance writer, having penned over 200 articles, devotions, and stories. Her work has appeared in publications by Focus on the Family, David C. Cook, Lifeway, Standard Publishing, *Chicken Soup for the Soul*, *The Upper Room*, Judson Press, Bethany House, and more. She also loves speaking to women's groups and teaching workshops on freelance writing.

She and her husband of more than 40 years

have four children and two grandchildren. When not writing, she enjoys substituting at a Christian school near her home, gardening, cooking, and traveling.

**Follow her on:**

**Facebook:** /harrietmichaelauthor

**Blog:** www.harrietemichael.blogspot.com

**Amazon:** /author/harrietemichael

# Also by the Authors

The Prayer Project
by Harriet and Shirley

# Non-Fiction from Entrusted Books

In this first book in the "Hope Rising Bible Series," Andrea Thom digs deep into the truths found in the book of Ruth. Her discoveries encourage women seeking meaning from difficult times and direction in the path on which the Lord has placed them.

Every week across America, single members filter into their local congregations to worship, minister, and serve alongside their brothers and sisters in Christ. Pastors and church leaders, many long married, often find themselves ill-equipped to understand the particular relational, emotional, and spiritual needs of long-term Christian singles. Worse, they're unaware that they're underequipped. Married church members, though sympathetic to the needs of their single friends, nevertheless struggle to bridge the divide.

Written by a dedicated Christ-follower and long-term Christian single, The Proper Care and Feeding of Singles addresses the issues with humor and grace, offering practical solutions to strengthen the bonds of love and fellowship within local congregations.

Thank you
for reading our books!

If you enjoyed this devotional,
please consider returning to its
purchase page and leaving a review!

Look for other books
published by

Entrusted Books
an Imprint of
Write Integrity Press

www.WriteIntegrity.com

Made in USA - Kendallville, IN
1099547_9781951602048
05.05.2020 0923